THE DARK SIDE OF THE HUMAN NEEDS

HELP CLIENTS ANSWER THE QUESTION 'WHY DO I DO THAT?' AND STOP SELF SABOTAGE

MARK TYRRELL

uncommon knowledge

The Dark Side of the Human Needs: Help Clients Answer the Question 'Why Do I Do That?' and Stop Self Sabotage

First Publication 2018

ISBN: 978-1-902892-36-8 EPUB
ISBN: 978-1-902892-35-1 paperback

Uncommon Knowledge Ltd
Boswell House,
Argyll Square
Oban
PA34 4BD

www.unk.com
support@unk.com

+44 (0) 1273 776770

CONTENTS

INTRODUCTION

Evil exists. At least, it certainly feels that way for those at the short end of abuse, crime, or genocide. People can and do sometimes treat one another in ways that could be described as evil.

But it seems that people can also do evil to themselves, if not intentionally then certainly as a side effect of their actions. One thing I've noticed, and perhaps you have too, is that when people sabotage their *own* lives, the (often unintended) consequences of the self-sabotage are negative for those around them as well.

The mother who marries an abusive man because her self-esteem is so poor may inflict harm on her children by exposing them to him. The work colleagues of the chronic drinker may constantly find themselves having to cover for him. The family of an inveterate gambler may face poverty and shame because of the resulting loss of family resources.

Two things are clear. Actions, *all* actions, have consequences and individual actions affect others in a ripple effect.

Some people will sabotage the lives of others to meet what they feel are their real needs. *Some* people sabotage their *own* lives through the hopeless entanglements of addiction or some compulsive behaviour.

Some people reject perfectly good relationships, some people are prepared to put up with abuse from others, even seem to *choose* relationships with those who are mean to them. Other people are hard to be around because of the way they interact socially. The hyper needy types often end up lonely as others find them "hard work." This rejection may, make them in turn, more needy and so the vicious cycle moves on.

Historically, and still in some places in the World I'm sad to say, some people will kill, enslave and destroy those around them. These people may have even be led to believe they are doing *good!*

But why does all this happen?

Why, and I'm not talking about the tiny minority of predatory psychopaths here, do perfectly reasonable people do terrible things to themselves and others?

When we understand why we can avoid falling in to the traps of life. And we can help other people escape these traps once they've fallen into them.

In this book on the dark side of the primal human needs, I will be looking at sometimes quite extreme examples of so called human evil. We'll look at cults such as the Jonestown mass suicide and the horrors of Nazi and communist death camps. But I'll also be seeking to unravel the core reasons why people, all of us, can be prone to messing our *own* lives up.

What prompted the creation of this book for me was the realization that all behaviour, however cruel, self defeating or warped is *purposeful.* When we start to look at what those, often unconscious, purposes might be, vistas of clarity open up before us. We come to better understand the sometimes bizarre and baffling behavior of those around us and ourselves.

I think this is a fascinating adventure for the mind and I hope you love this book as much as I did creating it.

But I also want it to be a practical guide for you. I hope it can help you navigate your own life better and, if you see clients, to help you better understand and help those who come to you seeking clarity and hope.

We'll look at what goes wrong when our needs for attention, safety, control, intimacy, connection to others, status, challenge, the needs of the mind and body and a sense of meaning are thwarted and subverted in ways which seem to produce what might be seen as "evil" outcomes. Or at least cause us and those around us harm.

It seems to me that personal development of individuals as much as humanity itself depends not merely on what we do but the traps we learn to *avoid.*

I hope this book goes a small way toward providing some kind of a road map to the avoidance of huge amounts of pain.

Mark Tyrrell
Co-founder
Uncommon Knowledge

CHAPTER ONE
ATTENTION

HOW YOU CAN BE MANIPULATED THROUGH YOUR NEED FOR ATTENTION

I heard a story once.

Long before mobile phones were a thing, a group of people were driving through a desert in punishing heat. As terrible luck would have it, their vehicle broke down, right there in the baking wilderness.

They were stranded for days and, drop by drop, their water supplies ran out.

Slowly, they began to die of dehydration.

One man eventually become so deliriously thirsty that he succumbed. He drank engine oil from their vehicle. He drank so much that he died.

Not half an hour later the others, weak and dehydrated beyond belief, were rescued and given fresh water.

The man who drank engine oil had a need. A real, undeniable need. He *felt* he was meeting it somehow, but the effects were deadly.

True or not, this tale is a perfect analogy for how emotional needs can make us just as vulnerable and drive us to just-as-crazy actions. And that's what this book is all about.

Why did I DO that?!

Why did I start smoking? Guzzle cake all night? Fall for that conniving conman? Willingly kill myself just because the cult I'd joined told me to do it?

How could I have been so stupid?

Why *do* otherwise rational human beings do crazy things? This book on the dark side of human emotional needs seeks to answer just this question, and to show you how you can use this understanding to help your clients, enrich the lives of those around you, and, most importantly, make sure you are meeting your *own* needs.

In this first piece, I want to give you an idea of how a thwarted *need for attention* can ruin lives.

Mysterious motivations

We all have basic, primal emotional needs. (These needs are central to understanding Human Givens Psychology.) When we meet these needs healthily, in a place where satisfying them won't cause problems, we have *spare capacity* to make good judgements and pursue long-term objectives. We have space in our emotional lives to work for a wider cause than the self, or to improve the self in the long term.

The healthy fulfilment of emotional needs is at the core of good mental health. There's no doubt that understanding emotional needs helps us be better practitioners.

As a reminder, all people, everywhere, to varying degrees, have a need:

- to give and receive attention
- to feel safe and secure
- to heed the mind–body connection
- to have a sense of purpose and meaning
- to feel a sense of connection to community and of making a difference
- to be stretched, to be creative, and to face manageable challenges
- to experience intimacy
- to feel a sense of control
- to feel a sense of status; to feel valued, appreciated, and respected.

When we are not meeting our emotional needs enough and in the right way, we are said to be *vulnerable*.

Lonely hearts beware

Lonely people – people who don't give and receive enough attention, have a sense of meaningful interaction (intimacy), or feel part of a group – become *vulnerable* because these needs remain unmet.

People who are unable or find it difficult to meet their needs, perhaps due to environmental factors or a condition such as autism, are vulnerable. And vulnerable people are very prone to depressing when they ruminate on their needs remaining unfulfilled.

Such people, those whose emotional needs are not met adequately, become so vulnerable to their own emotional drives that they, like the man in my opening analogy, may 'drink petrol'.

They can also be vulnerable to the influence of people who seem to give the person what they need emotionally, at least at first, but are unscrupulous. There's a reason so-called 'lonely hearts killers' target lonely people: they know their victims are so desperately searching for water that they might just drink petrol.

Let them drink! (But not all from the same glass)

Psychotherapists work to help their clients meet their needs in balance in their life. They help their clients remove what may have been blocking the completion of these needs.

And, to avoid clients becoming dependent on therapy, they help their clients meet these needs in a self-sustaining way *outside* of therapy. Therapy sessions can be thought of as 'training wheels' – they support the client until they are ready to discard them.

We help our clients meet their needs in a range of ways so they don't 'put all their eggs in one basket'. Having all or most emotional needs met by a single source is very dangerous. If that source disappears, everything falls to the ground. We call this the 'all your eggs in one basket trap'.

When people whose emotional needs are not being adequately met find themselves in a situation that *can* meet all their needs, they are likely to become dependent on that one person or organization.

This leaves them open to being more easily *manipulated* because they unconsciously *know* that all or most of their needs are being met through this person or organization. They hand over all power to that entity, and in the process lose their own claim to control. The fear of abandonment may become overwhelming as they come to feel that their needs can *only* be met by that one source.

Many of us are very careful to avoid being manipulated by others, but neglect to realize that we can just as easily be manipulated by our own emotional drives (which focus us on meeting emotional needs).

And when other people, instinctively or otherwise, twig which of our needs are under-met, they might make a point of focusing on *supplying* that need. They become your *supplier* of attention, or life meaning, or self-esteem.

But if they are your *sole* supplier, and you come to believe these needs cannot be met in any other way (perhaps because they told you this), then we have a problem. And this problem is all the more dangerous if they, be they a cult or a person, are controlling and unscrupulous.

I'll get back to this. But first I want to emphasize why understanding the attention factor in human life is so important.

Knowledge is *real* power

Knowledge is *real* power. And that's something we all need. Power to chart our own course in life.

When we are clear about our emotional needs, we see clearly why we develop emotional problems, and therefore how to avoid them as far as possible. But we also have an incredibly valuable tool to explain all kinds of otherwise baffling human behaviours.

Our needs are always seeking completion. Even when you're not aware that a need exists, it is still driving you. And it's driving you hard. Even when you think you're doing one thing, you might really be doing another.

So let's look at the need for attention and how it can work against us (and, of course, our clients).

When we don't even realize what we're doing

We all know people who demand more than their fair share of attention. They talk at length and expect you to listen, yet when *you* talk they can't seem to keep their focus. Every time you manage to squeeze a few words in, they are itching to snatch back the attention, and using what little time *you* get to rehearse what *they* will say next.

The natural, reciprocal back-and-forth flow of attention just doesn't seem to happen. You could be any old giant ear sitting there – in fact, an ear might be preferable. At least it can't interrupt.

People like this can be hard to be around, at least until they have 'drunk' enough from the cup of attention to calm their inflamed need.

If someone keeps asking for reassurance or 'advice' but never actually heeds it, then they're not asking for advice. They're seeking your attention. It's harder for someone to say, "I am seeking attention" than "Can I have your advice?" Besides, they may genuinely believe they are seeking advice. Self-knowledge isn't easy.

The best psychologist is the one who can see what people (and they themselves) are *actually* doing, not what they *say* they are doing.

Different personalities at different times require different quantities and qualities of attention. Some may not care what kind of attention they elicit, good or bad, while others may want approval and fear being seen negatively. On the flip side, the need for privacy or 'me time' may be indicative of a need for *less* attention.

The need for attention reaches just about every part of human life.

You may have heard of the Hawthorne Effect, named after

a study done in the 1920s and '30s in which workers in a factory were observed to see what changes in working conditions would increase their happiness and productivity.

After many external changes to their working environment, it was concluded it was the interest and *attention* the workers received from the researchers that made them happier and better workers, not the conditions themselves. Attention is powerful.

The need for attention is honest in babies who simply cry for it. Unfortunately, if I go to a party and feel I'm not getting enough attention, I can't really start hollering and screaming to gain the attention I feel is my right (at least, not until the seventh pint of beer!).

Adults (well, most of them) are more sophisticated than babies, and may be able to find subtle and complex ways to meet their 'nutritional' need for attention. The trouble is, if we don't meet it in ways that are healthy, we become less effective and cause ourselves and others problems.

You may have met people who are extremely vocal about some cause or other. They rant and rave about how close it is to their heart, yet you can't help but wonder – if suddenly they ceased gaining any attention for espousing this cause, would they continue with it just as passionately? Or is this cause, so 'close to their heart', actually an unconscious device for gaining attention?

You might say it doesn't matter as long as they are doing good. But that view neglects to take into account personal effectiveness and spare capacity.

How to be an effective human being

The well-worn analogy for this is the man who hasn't eaten for a week but believes his primary need and focus is to learn

Spanish at night school.

He attends his evening class, but the whole time he is thinking about, asking about, and looking for not a broadening of his Spanish vocabulary, but the one thing his body knows it needs – food. He may say, and even *think* his interest is Spanish, but that's not what his drive really is.

Because his basic need hasn't been met elsewhere, he can't help but demand its completion within the current realm – one in which it really shouldn't apply. He stops himself from being fully effective at learning Spanish. Worse still, he may stop other students from learning too.

This idea of getting your house in order *before* you strive for higher, non-basic, long-term aims is really important for all of us to register.

It's quite an ancient idea. Centuries ago, it was a requirement for certain types of spiritual activity that the applicant for study be meeting his or her emotional needs *before* they could seek higher fulfilment. Otherwise, the spiritual activity could be considered tantamount to an emotionally based cult. (See *The Commanding Self*, by Idries Shah).

But you'll notice there is a bit of a cultural taboo against this idea, and for many it is quite unfamiliar. Many people seem to reject the 'spare capacity' idea out of hand. But if you *use* the idea, it can transform your life. And, of course, your clients' lives.

There are other ways the drive for attention can cause people problems, both emotional and social, and block personal progress:

- The untamed drive for attention can cause us to seek attention, be it good or bad. Not receiving, or being able to give, healthy attention at home may cause a child to seek it at school. Disapproval is still attention (eventually, when we want not just any but a certain kind of attention, we may say we want 'respect', although for some the word respect has been misinterpreted to mean 'fear'.)

- Some people may get a kind of 'secondary gain' from the attention their emotional or behavioural problem elicits. They may, perhaps unconsciously, fear they will lose a source of attention, perhaps a partner or friends, if they 'get better' – especially if the problem has been longstanding. Attention may need to be withdrawn from one area (the problematic behaviour) and extended to more positive aspects of the person's life.
- While someone is starving for attention, this need may become so urgent it ironically *prevents* them forming social ties which, if formed, would be a healthy supply of the attention need.

All things in balance

It isn't that we shouldn't meet any of our attention needs from activities that aren't ostensibly social. But if following the cause or the learning or any other activity is *mainly* an unconscious vehicle for attention, then:

- We will be less effective than if we had a 'clean slate' or spare capacity from the need being adequately met elsewhere. Our decisions may be predicated on "How much attention does this give me?" rather than "What is best for the wider cause?"
- We may lose interest if the perhaps worthwhile activity stops giving us attention in the same

> measure. For instance, someone may lose interest in their healthy eating plan once others habituate to their slimmer, healthier appearance and therefore give them less attention in that way. If their motivation was *mainly* to do with eliciting approval, then they may go back to unhealthy eating unless they can find another motivation, such as being healthier for themselves and themselves alone.

So to be really effective we need to meet our attention needs in ways that don't interfere with our activities.

Imagine a practitioner, maybe someone naturally communicative and sociable, who *never* saw anyone in their lives other than their clients. The practitioner may well have no spare capacity to be effective *for the client*. They may feel the overriding 'thirst' to talk about themselves to the client non-stop.

So helping clients and ourselves *understand* the central role the exchange of attention plays is vital. We can then help regulate it to become happier, healthier, and more effective.

And of course the attention factor plays a major role in human relationships. If someone is starving for attention, or seeking it all from only one place, they may develop real problems, from stalking to feeling suicidal, if a relationship breaks down.

Many friends, many social contacts, and at least a few social events a month all help create spare capacity so that we don't turn everything we do into a disguised attempt at meeting this most basic of needs.

But not meeting the attention need also leaves us vulnerable to a kind of psychological attack (not to sound too melodramatic!).

Let's look at this another way for a moment.

Pushing the self-destruct button

One way to understand subtle psychological influence is to clearly see more gross psychology at work.

It's 1978, in Guyana. There you stand, in the middle of 'Jonestown', a loyal member of Jim Jones' cult: 'The People's Temple'. He commands you, along with 900 others, to take poison and die. What do you do?

Well, of course you don't do it. Who is *he* to tell you to end it all? You are not an automaton to be ordered about!

But an astounding 900 people simply followed his instructions. People who wanted to live, and wanted their children and wives and husbands to live.

Why did they do it? Why did all these men and women allow themselves to be sexually abused and Pied-Pipered all the way to an early tomb? Why did they agree to sell their homes and give all their money to the People's Temple? Were they of unusually low intelligence? Were they completely crazy? All of them?

Or was Jim Jones a highly skilled manipulator of human emotionality? Did he instinctively know how to push the human 'buttons' and so string people along, even to the extent that they would poison their own children?

Before the implosion of his cult, Jim Jones had expertly sought to meet all his followers' emotional needs through him and him alone. The power of a cult lies in the fact that it prevents you meeting your needs from anywhere but itself. Relatives and friends not in the cult are derided, and you may be denied access to them.

The message from a cult or charming manipulator is "You can only meet your needs from me! Without me you are nothing! Only I can give you love, meaning, connection, purpose, and ultimate safety!"

One technique 'The People's Temple' used was to shower new recruits with attention and approval – 'love bombing'. People without purpose, who felt marginalized (which means not gaining an adequate sense of attention from wider society) or lonely, were suddenly given undivided focus.

If you are dying of thirst and someone gives you water, and *only they seem to be able to provide that water*, you might feel you would do anything they say. You or I might have ended our time in Jonestown in 1978, too.

But 'love bombing' is used as much by individuals as groups.

Meeting of your needs, or just manipulation?

Any organization or unscrupulous person will, if they are to manipulate you, do it through your emotional needs. They will seem to offer you the easy completion of many of your emotional and even physical needs.

And for someone whose needs *aren't* being met adequately this can be overwhelming.

You might ask: "What does she *see* in him!?"

A better question is: "What does he seem to give her and how can she otherwise meet that need?"

I have worked with both women and men recovering from tumultuous and traumatic relationships with narcissistic manipulators.

Here are the kinds of things I have heard hundreds of times:

"At first he showered me with affection. He was so attentive. It was all about me. It was overwhelming!"

"I was new to the area and didn't know many people. He seemed so besotted with me. He would text me 20 times a day, send me flowers and tell me he loved me. That's before it became a nightmare."

"I had gone through a really hard divorce and was feeling bad about who I was. She made me feel fantastic! Told me I was wonderful, was constantly affectionate, told me that she loved me every day, really suckered me in!"

Love bombing – attention overdose

People can be left feeling stupid when it happens to them, but love bombing is such an intense form of supplying such a basic need that none of us are immune to it.

Love bombing happens in cohesive organizations to hook the potential member and hold them fast. It also happens on the personal level and masquerades as genuine romance.

The love bomber would be instinctively skilled at spotting which needs – and there may be many – are not being met adequately, and seeming to meet those needs in overwhelming abundance so that the object of the love bombing becomes 'stuck on them', and therefore malleable.

Before you write me off as a romanceless cynical old hack, I want to make it clear that some people *are* incredibly romantic, and do like to shower their lover with attention and loving gestures in a genuine way without then going on to destroy their lives.

What I really mean is that overdosing someone with attention is also a way of emotionally destabilizing them to the point that they become yours to own.

One way to discover whether a relationship is toxic to the extent that it has become essentially a 'cult of two people' is to consider whether the love bomber is unreasonably demanding ("after all I do for you!") or resents you meeting your attention needs outside of the relationship. Has the love bombing become demand-napalm?

One woman told me, "Pretty soon he tried to stop me seeing my friends and family. He would say horrible things about them!"

Any cult will want to be the *sole* source of influence on you. Even if there's just the two of you in the cult.

So to summarize this brief exploration of the flow of the human need for attention:

- The giving and receiving of attention is a vital human need. When the need is not met people suffer mentally and eventually even physically.[1]
- Being too desperate for attention can make it, ironically, harder to build the relationships that might become a stable source for the completion of this fundamental need. A neat but horrible vicious circle.
- If we don't meet our attention needs in social ways or within familiar settings, the need may build and seep out to pollute other enterprises. This makes us less effective. If we start to receive less attention for a particular (maybe worthwhile) activity, we may quickly lose interest in the political cause, or diet, or whatever the overt goal of the activity was, once we no longer receive the same levels of attention from it.
- Meeting our needs for attention adequately helps us build *spare capacity* within ourselves to actually focus on bigger patterns and long-term goals. Once you've eaten, you have a better shot at learning Spanish.
- There may be an attention-seeking element to

problematic feelings and behaviours. Disapproval can be a very focused and powerful form of attention from others.

- Occasionally someone may derive a 'secondary gain' from maintaining a long-term problem, in the form of ongoing attention from a partner or others. Conversely, some partners may worry that once their loved one gets better they will no longer be needed. The need to be needed is part of the attention need too.
- Finally, if someone is chronically undernourished with attention they may be susceptible to 'love bombing' from organizations and/or individuals who, like Venus flytraps, seem to offer when they really seek to take.

The attention factor in all human life is fascinating, and understanding when and how it operates can help us know ourselves and others better. It's too easy to say, "I know attention is important... duh!" or words to that effect. But when you start seeing how the drive for attention influences so much of human life, all kinds of seemingly bizarre behaviour becomes easier to understand.

I hope you've enjoyed my first foray into the dark side of the human needs. In the next chapter I'll be exploring the dark side of the need to feel safe and secure.

Let me leave you with this quote from the English writer William Hazlitt:

> "The art of conversation is the art of hearing as well as of being heard."

CHAPTER TWO
SAFETY

HOW THE NEED TO FEEL SAFE AND SECURE CAN LEAD TO CHRONIC ANXIETY, PEOPLE-PLEASING, AND COULD LAND YOU IN A CULT

"If you see me as your friend, I'll be your friend. If you see me as your father, I'll be your father... If you see me as your saviour, I'll be your saviour. If you see me as your God, I'll be your God."

JIM JONES

"How could something that started out with such good intentions end so badly?"

CHRIS SAUNDERS, *THE DEATH OF JIM JONES AND PEOPLES TEMPLE*

A man hides away for years because he only feels safe in his own house. A sportswoman panics when she forgets her 'lucky socks' for the big tournament. A teenager refuses to go anywhere unless she knows her 'escape' route. A middle-aged man washes his hands a thousand times a day.

There's no doubt about it. We humans can be intensely irrational, even when it leads to self-sabotage. Or complete annihilation!

In Chapter 1 of this book I explained that attention is a kind of vital nutrient – one we all need to varying degrees – but that our need for it can also poison us.

Not only can our unconscious drive to meet our need for attention *in the wrong area* stop us from achieving our dreams (because gaining attention is the true hidden priority), it can also be used by unscrupulous people to wreak havoc on our lives. 'Love bombing', as I wrote, is powerful.

In this chapter, I'm going to look at how the drive to feel safe and secure can also work against our clients (and us!). If misdirected, this drive can lead us to seek a sense of safety in ways that, paradoxically, undermine our very existence.

Uncontrolled unconscious drives

Our primal emotional needs drive much of our unconscious behaviour. This book is about bringing that unconscious behaviour into the conscious domain. It's about knowing what our – and our clients' – needs are, being clear about them, and understanding the dangers of trying to 'meet the need for hydration by drinking engine oil'.

Meeting our needs in balance keeps us sane and safe. Safe from the kind of manipulation I'll be addressing here.

The need to feel safe is paramount. I'm not saying all adversity should be avoided, or that we should be so 'safe spaced' from contrary opinions that we end up soft, brittle, and fragile. I just mean we need to feel secure *enough* to have the spare capacity not just to survive life, but to embrace it.

At its deepest level, the drive for safety and security is really the drive for survival itself. In more primitive times, a lack of shelter and safety meant there was no guarantee you'd live to see the next day. No wonder we still have such an inherent drive to feel safe and secure.

The primal drive for security may help us protect ourselves in some situations, but it can also trip us up in modern life.

Safety first

In Chapter 1, I made the point that when people are starved of attention they don't feel safe. That's because once upon a time loneliness, living away from the tribe, was *literally* dangerous.

And so was exposure. Finding shelter meant we were *safe*, if only for the moment. We could continue to exist. When we began farming, it meant increased *security*. We knew where our next meal (and many more after that) was coming from.

In modern life, fulfilment of this need relates to financial security, healthcare and physical safety. It relates to the fulfilment of our other basic emotional and physical needs. It relates to trusting relationships. It relates to being able to plan ahead and have a sense of how things will be: the opposite of uncertainty.

All this helps us feel more secure and frees us up to focus on aspects of life beyond survival.

But what happens when people try to meet the drive for safety in ways that actually work *against* them?

Fear, anxiety, panic, and obsession...

All fear and anxiety conditions, including panic attacks, generalized anxiety disorder, obsessive compulsive disorder and post-traumatic stress disorder, are manifestations of the same need: the need to feel safe and secure.

Rather than seeing these conditions as pathological, we

could view them as sloppy, maladaptive unconscious attempts at meeting primal emotional needs.

But even if we don't suffer to *that* extent with anxiety, we can all fall victim to a misdirected drive to seek safety and security.

... meanness, timidity, and depression

Chronic meanness when someone *has* the resources to be generous may be a kind of – and here I'm going to use a very old-fashioned word (trigger warning!) – cowardice.

Feeling we can't spend money, or 'waste' money, may signify an overwhelming drive to feel safe and secure. The meanest people I've known have tended to be pretty wealthy. Yes, that might help explain their wealth... but when is enough money enough?

Likewise, an excessive drive for safety and security may produce a kind of chronic timidity in which life is *never* taken by the horns, no risks are taken and no challenges are faced. Yes, avoidance may be safe, but so is being dead. Not daring to try carries its own risks. Regret and resentment aren't great comforters as life moves on.

As practitioners we need to help our clients find ways to meet this fundamental need healthily. Indeed, much of what we do *does* require us to help our clients feel safer. A huge part of depression treatment is about helping our clients feel safe again, to begin to move in life and meet their needs sustainably.

In fact, a myriad of different symptoms common to our caseload relate to the innate drive towards security.

From chronic reassurance-seeking to horrific flashbacks

Incessant worrying; chronic washing, checking or counting; flashbacks; panic attacks; addiction to alcohol or opiates and 'comfort eating' are all ways in which the unconscious mind may desperately seek a sense of safety.

Even depression, in which energy shuts down and basic challenges are avoided, can be seen as a kind of unconscious retreat into a dark cave that the light of day can't reach.

Some people become such rule-bound lovers of bureaucratic processes that spontaneity and common sense don't even seem to factor into the equation. Chronic rule-following may also be an attempt at feeling secure. An attempt at 'covering all the bases'.

All these can be viewed as maladaptive attempts to feel safe and secure. But of course, they don't work.

If we look at what need any behaviour or emotional condition is trying to meet then just about all facets of the human condition become explicable.

People who seek reassurance or approval are really seeking to meet their need for a sense of safety and security. People who can't stand the unexpected or a break from routine are really seeking a sense of security.

When we feel unsafe we are, by definition, in seeking mode. We are constantly *looking* for safety. And when we are desperate, we are easily led. What *seems* to offer us safety may, in fact, be poison.

When people become parasites

> *"Parasite, noun: 1. An organism that lives in or on another organism (its host) and benefits by deriving nutrients at the other's expense."*
>
> GOOGLE DICTIONARY

Hitler offered safety and security (and dignity) to the German people. Eventually, it became objectively unsafe *not* to follow him.

Stalin, murderer of millions, also offered a kind of utopia... at first.

And I won't even talk about the wonderful promises of freedom and safety Communist leader Chairman Mao Tse-tung made before killing an estimated 45 million of his own people.

"Let me be leader of your tribe and I will offer peace, security, comfort, and self-respect. With me you are safe!" This is the timeless message of those who would exploit our trust and squander our lives.

The machinations of a cult can occur in groups of any size, from an entire nation to, I would suggest, just two people.

Captivating cults

Cults promise:

- Safety (be cast out and be damned!)
- Meaning
- Togetherness
- Feelings of being special or 'chosen'.

Cults also:

- Devalue outsiders
- Shout down dissent
- Alternate hope with fear
- Seek to convince members that only the cult can meet their needs. The sole provider becomes the sole source of ideas, and demands for 'payback' abound.

All abusive relationships have cult-like elements. They meet needs in the short term but become parasitical fast.

But there are more subtle ways we can convince ourselves we are safe.

Ideological safety

Wanting to feel we are 'ethical', and therefore that others are less so, may also be indicative of a drive to feel secure. After all, feeling righteous is a way of feeling safe in the knowledge that "I am good."

When this kind of safety is promised – "we are good; others are not!" – the end can so easily come to justify the means. The safety offered by one-size-fits-all ideologies leads people to engage in terrible collective behaviours, convinced they are 'necessary' for the 'greater good'.

The drive for security is so potent that we can be taken in by anyone who seems to offer certainty. In this way, 'security' and 'certainty' are virtually interchangeable.

'Safety in numbers' is tempting, but as Stalin eventually put it: "A single death is a tragedy; a million deaths is a statistic."

The drive for money is so often a drive for safety too.

A more modern form of safety

Our need to feel safe and secure, just like our need for attention, permeates and secretly influences all areas of life. It can certainly affect our financial life.

Some people want money to increase status, to show off or to have and do nice things. But many want money because it represents safety. "I have enough nuts and berries to survive the winter."

We want to feel safe. We lock money in 'safes'. We invest in 'trusts' (and we only trust when we feel safe).

This is exactly what scammers play on. They know that if they can gain our trust, they can gain our money. When we feel safe, we become less vigilant. To revert once more to primitive terms, it is as if the cave is secure, and we are in it with someone we trust. We think, "I'll give my food to this person for safekeeping. I can *tell* they will not only look after it but *add* to it."

If our drive for safety is too desperate, we may stop thinking.

Many financial scammers are organized and businesslike. But they can be far more covert than that. Malcolm's story shows just how easily we can come to trust those who mean us harm.

My vulnerable and wealthy client

Malcolm met Trisha in a bar.

"She was all over me from the get-go! [Alarm bells, anyone?] I told her I had all kinds of issues with anxiety, but she didn't mind. She helped me overcome my panic. She cared for me [Malcolm was grieving after the death of a child] and made me feel so safe and secure..."

That really struck me. Somehow this woman must have

picked up – quickly, skilfully, and imperceptibly – that Malcolm was that perfect combination of vulnerable and wealthy.

"She would calm me down, tell me silly little stories, soothe me. She was like the mother I never had."

Somehow I knew a hefty "but" was about to fall.

And there it was.

"But I kept losing money. There'd be £100 in my wallet when she arrived, and the next day it would be gone. But I turned a blind eye because I felt I couldn't lose her."

Trisha had made Malcolm feel so safe he felt he *couldn't lose her* – but he was losing money. Fast.

He related his torturous tale. Trisha had defrauded him out of £25,000, slept with other men, constantly told him that without her he would be "nothing" and, when he finally felt it might be safer *not* to be with her, tried to ruin his reputation at work and on social media.

He ended up taking out an injunction and at last she left him alone. Finally, he was rescued from his 'rescuer'.

I sought to reassure him that he hadn't been "stupid", as he said, but that he had simply judged her by his own standards of behaviour. I also suggested that she had picked up on his primary emotional need, and seemed to meet it (at first).

A parasite contorting itself to fit the host.

Helping our clients find real, sustainable safety

We can all get sucked in by the dynamics of our needs. Some people and organizations can make us feel safer, but we need to be wary of the wolf in a sheepskin coat.

What problematic behaviours and feelings in your clients relate to the need to feel secure? *Why* doesn't the client feel safe? What is stopping them feeling secure? And how can their need for safety and security be *authentically* met so that they needn't look for it in the wrong places?

When we help our clients meet their needs in sustainable ways, comfortably lift trauma, and equip our clients with ways to stop panic attacks before they get started, we help them feel naturally safer. Learning to calm ourselves and others is vital too, and part of that involves becoming better at relaxing with uncertainty.

When we don't feel safe we can become so frightened we lose the capacity to think clearly or make good judgements. The more we can all learn how the need to feel safe can be subverted, the healthier we will all be.

CHAPTER THREE
CONTROL

HOW THE NEED TO FEEL A SENSE OF CONTROL CAN LEAD TO BROKEN RELATIONSHIPS, POLITICAL TYRANNY, AND DEPRESSION

"If everything seems under control, you're just not going fast enough."

MARIO ANDRETTI, RACING DRIVER

What can you control in your life?

Your health? What others think of you? How happy your lover is? The weather? Your finances? Your future? Your appearance? Your mood? Other people's moods?

Can you control these things completely, or just influence them to *some* extent?

Some folk feel that they should have 100% control, others that they have none at all.

We've looked at how, when people's needs remain chronically unmet, they become vulnerable not just to mental illness but also to manipulation by the unscrupulous.

"How did she fall for that conniving conman?" Well, maybe he *seemed* to meet an unmet need in her life. "How did he fall for that murderous cult?" Likewise, it seemed to offer something that had been chronically lacking.

Promises, promises.

To rehash the analogy I've been using throughout this book, if you're dying of thirst, you might just drink engine oil!

In this piece I want to talk about how the desire to feel in control can work – and be *used* – against us.

One thing's for sure, we all need *some* sense of control.

The need for dignity – or is it control?

We often equate self-direction and autonomy with words like 'dignity' – a word which, when you unpack it, really means control over one's decisions and actions.

The controversial clinic in Switzerland where some terminally ill people have chosen to end their lives *on their terms* is actually called 'Dignitas'. It offers the ultimate control – to choose when and where you die!

When elderly people in nursing homes are allowed to make more choices, even minor ones, they have better psychological outcomes and even longevity.[1]

Having a sense of control matters to everyone. Whether you realize it or not, you've been seeking to develop and exert control since the moment you were born.

Hardwired to self-determine

From the second we're born we seek autonomy, independence, and control. We strive to control what we do, the effect others have on us, and the effect we have on others. Even the urges to walk, speak, and play all are partly driven by the desire for independence.

A major parental role is to facilitate independence in their child so they can function and meet their and other people's needs when they develop into adults.

Adults who feel at least some sense of realistic control tend to be much happier, which is why we need to look at how in or out of control our clients feel. And science has some interesting findings on this.

A healthy dose of control

A recent study found that having a strong sense of control over your circumstances reduces the risk of dying prematurely by 13 percent![2]

Other research has shown that higher perceived control in adolescents is linked to lower psychological stress, better cardio-vascular health, lower systemic inflammation, and reduced obesity by the time those adolescents reach young adulthood.[3]

In turn, the healthy decisions that result from perceived control can lead to favourable outcomes much later in life. From pain sensitivity[4] to the onset and maintenance of depression[5], how able (or unable) we feel to control our lives has far-reaching impacts.

But here's the most interesting thing.

It's just good to know you *could* exert control

Even just knowing you *could* control things seems to make a big difference.

I recall seeing some research (although I couldn't find it!) which showed that patients who were permitted to self-administer morphine for pain relief used much less than those who had to ask others to provide it.

This quote from Wikipedia describes similar results from another study[6]:

> "[I]*n one experiment humans performed mental tasks in the presence of distracting noise. Those who could use a switch to turn off the noise rarely bothered to do so, yet they performed better than those who could not turn off the noise. Simply being aware of this option was enough to substantially counteract the noise effect.*"

Just *knowing* we have someone to talk to (whether or not we do), just *knowing* there are contingency plans in place (whether or not we use them), just *knowing* we can safely quit a job (whether or not we choose to) can make us happier.

Always be looking for options.

I will often ask my clients, "If the worst *did* happen, what are some things you could do?" In this way 'the end of the world' becomes the beginning of a new one.

But the need for control, just like all primal emotional needs, is so powerful that our drive to meet it can cause huge problems.

The dark side of the need for control

Like all our emotional drives, the need for control can be warped and abused, and paradoxically lead to *less* control and even tyranny.

We can fall prey to those who seem to offer more control – individual or national 'dignity' – but, as if through a clever conjuring trick, end up taking control from us.

Maybe your clients feel overly passive, that life must be done for them, or that "no matter what I do, it doesn't make any difference!" Learned helplessness is the intimate bedfellow of hopelessness, which is a central feature of depression. Misdiagnosing what you can and can't control in your life has major impacts.

So why might people feel they are *less* able to control events that they really are?

Learning *not* to control

Learned helplessness is the *general* application of a *specific* learning. We feel powerless in one situation, so we come to feel powerless in *all* situations: "That accountant I dated was manipulative, therefore all accountants are manipulative."

But it's not just people who can learn to over-apply these feelings. Even animals can develop learned helplessness. Martin Seligman, who coined the term, found that humans and animals who learned they were helpless in one situation (because they really *couldn't* change things) would often over-apply that learned helplessness and not bother to try to change things *when now they could have.*

That's all very well, but in the non-experimental ebb and flow of human life, how might people learn the illusion of too little control? How might they develop a misperception so powerful that it may shape their whole life?

The need for rebellion

Over-controlling 'helicopter' parents (and institutions), despite the best of intentions, may pervert children's natural drive for autonomy.

I say the best of intentions, but of course if the unconscious drive of the parent is to keep the child dependent, we might question those intentions. Worst intentions *disguised* as best intentions are the most dangerous of all. After all, they are borne of love!

Parents (who I know get a lot of stick!) may mould children into overly dependent beings, keeping them infantilized –

sometimes indefinitely. Parents need to be protective, involved, and loving, but if the child can *never* have choices or take reasonable risks they may not develop a sense that they *can* direct things.

Often, depending on the child, there is a bounce-back effect. Something's got to give because the need for self-direction, for dignity, is so strong.

If the child doesn't rebel against 'helicoptering' they end up feeling that they can't influence their own lives. They may sink into passivity and powerlessness, feeling that life had better be kind to them because they have no control themselves.

Always doing everything for another person steals their dignity and breeds a hopeless and depressive mindset. If we can't trust ourselves to do things, then how can we develop a sense of control?

And a further trap may await the poor individual who has not learned to feel their own power.

Live with it because it's who you are!

The overly dependent person may come to feel even *less* control if they are caught in the ever-widening dragnet of psychiatric diagnosis.

Ironically, branding someone with a label like 'dependent personality disorder' can make them feel more dependent! When that label is applied confidently by an authority figure, it's hardly surprising that the diagnosed person may feel *more* powerless. After all if it's 'who you are' – hardwired – how could you possibly have the control to change it?

But there is another way to come to feel you are less in control than you really are.

Once bitten, twice shy

When a person who suffers intense and prolonged bullying, neglect, or abuse feels unable to exert any influence over adversity of other kinds they can be conditioned to feel that we, not our circumstances, are at the root of our powerlessness. I suggest ways to help clients overcome this overly applied learning here.

Imagine you have been caged for many years, and one day you are freed. But you can't bring yourself to leave the now wide-open door of the cage. That's what it's like for people with a powerless mindset.

Doing too much for a person can condition them into that mindset, as can prolonged adversity. Whatever the route to passivity, the result is often the same: depression and a sense of meaninglessness. As meaning-seeking, meaning-making creatures, this can feel like purgatory.

On the flip side of the coin, some people have the opposite problem: they may come to feel they should control all kinds of stuff which is none of their business to control.

Let me count the ways... I can control you!

Sometimes a need morphs into a greed. A simple and natural need for a good, healthy sense of control transforms into a need to dominate – in other words, hunger for power.

Some see others as chess pieces to be carefully placed to meet their own ends. For these people, the need to control has grown wings and begun napalming all those that populate their lives.

Rather than *interrelating* with others, they control and manipulate them to meet their *own* needs exclusively. We all might do this sometimes, but those who do it all the time have a serious problem.

Such people are sometimes referred to as narcissists, sociopaths, and/or 'control freaks'. They see the currency of human relationships as one of control only. This can be bemusing and confounding for the victim of such interactions who *doesn't* see all interaction as a power play.

So how might this pathological social control be exerted?

A person might exert control through force. The bellowing bully. The bull in a china shop steamroller (to spectacularly mix my metaphors). The frustrated, failed concentration camp commandant applicant.

But some controllers are more subtle. You might not even know you *have* been controlled until you spot the trend.

Some people bully you so nicely 'for your own good' you can forget that it *is* bullying. Others may control those around them more artfully through 'emotional blackmail', exercising control by playing the victim:

- "If you leave me [to go out for this one evening with your friends] I don't know *what* I'll do!"
- "After all I've done for you!"
- "No, you go out [sniff], I'll be fine [sniff], go and enjoy yourself!"

Emotional blackmailers control others quietly and subtly, all the while seeming to have no control.

Such attempts at controlling others often result when our ideas about how things must be are too tight.

Perilous perfectionism

Some people are perfectionists, rigid and brittle in the way they go about parts of their lives. Of course, many people can be like this *sometimes*, but for others it's an ongoing part of their personality – and it can cause real problems.

They know *exactly* how they want things, and unless you know too, boy are you in trouble!

Maladaptive perfectionism is the desire or need to control all kinds of things that, actually, we would do well to relax with *not* having to control. That need for a sense of control can get so out of hand that we can't keep up with it and, ironically, we end up feeling *less* in control.

So often the antidote lies in the development of the capacity to relax with uncertainty.

Of course, the feeling of wanting to control what may be none of our business to control doesn't have to be malicious. It can be done with the very best of intentions.

Often, people who overextend their sense of responsibility (control) are decent and caring people. They may feel responsible for all their friends' and neighbours' marriages (okay, perhaps I exaggerate mildly) or for *every little thing* to do with their grown children's lives.

People may try to control others by trying to make them feel guilty, by suggesting that the person they are targeting should have been able to control all kinds of things that they 'chose' not to. "You should have known I would be angry!"

When the need for control is subverted because it's not met healthily, all kinds of emotional problems can arise.

At least I can control *this*!

Occasionally I've seen clients who've told me they have, at one time, attempted suicide. One woman who had actually planned to kill herself said, "You know Mark... it's weird, but when I made the decision I felt better... like at least I could *do* something!"

This shows how vital the need for autonomy is and how, when people don't meet it healthily, it will try to find expression in unhealthy – even fatal – ways.

The thwarted need for control, along with the need to feel safe, might also drive psychological conditions such as:

- Depression (perfectionism has been linked to a much greater risk of suicide[7])
- Obsessive compulsive disorder
- Jealousy (we feel we should control the actions or even thoughts of the object of our focus)
- Eating disorders[8]
- Chronic anger

All these conditions seek to increase our sense of control but paradoxically can lead to feelings of loss of control.

And our individualistic culture doesn't always help as far as the personal control issue is concerned.

"You can do anything!"

Being reared with the idea that "you can be whatever you want to be!" can, paradoxically, be *dis*empowering.

Why? Because when the self-righteous waves of oversimplified fantasy crash against the unforgiving rocks of reality, the disappointment can be so great as to send people to the opposite pole, feeling that they can't be *anything* they want to be.

Human beings have been around for too long to still be peddling oversimplifications. Yes, we can do amazing things. But wanting isn't enough on its own. Knowledge, hard work and perseverance, personal predilection, and the flexibility to change course if things aren't working are also pretty useful!

Plus, the ideology of "I can be anything I want to be" is a slippery slope. It can so easily be directed toward others: "*You* can be anything I want *you* to be!"

Buying into the overly simplistic self-help ideas that everything, even disease, is down to what we want (and therefore under our control) is dangerous. On the other hand, learning how to relax with uncertainty, develop resilience, and be cool with ambiguity are capacities that really help people thrive.

So is a little bit of cynicism. Through the ages, many leaders have sucked people in with the promise of more control right before snatching it away.

Five simple steps to tyranny

> *"The Third Reich will always retain its right to control the owners of property."*
>
> ADOLF HITLER

> *"It is imperative to carry out merciless mass terror against the kulaks, priests and White Guards; unreliable elements are to be locked up in a concentration camp outside the town."*
>
> VLADIMIR LENIN

Without further ado, here they are: five simple steps to becoming a successful dictator.

1. Take one group, or nation, of people who don't feel much control
2. Raise the anger and bitterness levels to a greater pitch. Slowly bring to the boil
3. Sprinkle in some emotionally arousing promises of reclaiming dignity and control
4. Add a dash of expectation that *your* system will give the people greater control (and therefore dignity and status)
5. Finally, serve up your own power and take control from the very ones you promised it to.

Mind you, to serve up this dish you might need a (un)healthy dose of charisma – just like Hitler, or Stalin, or Jim Jones.

But if world domination isn't one of your hobbies, what about money?

Scammers (and I include cult leaders, though to be fair they may also be scamming themselves) often offer the chance at great riches.

Scam, scam, thank you ma'am!

We want more money because more money gives us more *control*.

We may feel that cashola increases our status, meaning we have more control over what (we believe) others think of us. One thing's for sure, it certainly increases our options. And the more options you have, the more control you have. Deciding *where* you go on vacation means more control than not being able to have one at all.

Equating money with more control is all very well, but the drive for this kind of control can become so acute that we can be left in ruins by the first person who seems to say: "Follow me and get rich quick!"

Our desire for money and status, and all the other goodies of life for that matter, can perhaps be traced to our initial attempts as infants to move and direct our own realities.

If you feel powerless – that you have little dignity or autonomy – then your increased 'hunger' for control *might* let you fall prey to any entity that seems to promise more.

The power play of life

Watch for power plays in everyday life. How do others seek to exert control in all the myriad subtle ways of doing it?

How many emotional problems, when we look at the pattern, are just misguided attempts to gain more control (in ways that backfire and make things worse for the person themselves as well as those around them)? How many puzzling or harmful behaviours are actually just cries for more control?

How in control do your clients feel? What parts of their life do they feel they can influence, and what parts not so much? How can we help them to increase their sphere of influence or relax the feeling that they *must* control stuff that they really don't have to?

It's not always easy to control ourselves, and sometimes it might *seem* easier to let others control us. To let *them* do the work. But we all need the power, control, and dignity to make at least *some* important choices for ourselves.

The trouble with handing over the steering wheel to

someone else is that your best interests may be the last thing on their minds, or in their hearts.

As Lao Tzu said:

> *"He who controls others may be powerful, but he who has mastered himself is mightier still."*

CHAPTER FOUR
INTIMACY

HOW THE NEED FOR LOVE AND INTIMACY CAN LEAD TO STALKING, ACCEPTING ABUSE AND IMPOSSIBLE RELATIONSHIPS

"Death is not the greatest loss in life. The greatest loss is what dies inside us while we live."

NORMAN COUSINS

Love! The spark that lights the fuse of life.

We all have a drive for intimacy. The mingling of your spirit with another's; a merging of souls, both physically and emotionally. Real intimacy brings both transcendent sympathy and urgent attraction. You fit together even in your differences. Your shameful little habits and idiosyncrasies are not just tolerated, but loved!

The concept of having met the person seems foreign; it's as if somehow, some way, you've known one another all along. The tiresome charades and pretenses of life melt away; suddenly you feel more 'real'. True intimacy is like coming home to the heart of all things.

How atavistically wonderful. How womb-like. How glowingly safe... yet exciting.

Make no mistake, the drive for intimacy is a mighty powerful one. And some have a greater appetite for love than others.

But if real gold exists then so does false gold. And any strong drive, when thwarted, subverted, or perverted, can cause problems – potentially fatal problems.

So what happens when that drive works (or is worked) against us?

"Our special time!"

Back in the day, when I was still young and working in a psychiatric hospital, patients would sit in the TV room after dinner. The air was oppressive, thick with cigarette smoke, but if you squinted hard enough you could just make out the screen through the haze.

As a junior (this was early days), I was often told to sit with the patients while they watched TV. Some patients were depressed, some were recovering alcoholics, and some were, or had been, psychotic. Audrey fell into the latter category.

Audrey was in love.

Not with me, I hasten to add, but with the twinkle-eyed Irish talk show host and raconteur Terry Wogan.

Sir Terry (he would later be knighted) graced British TV screens three evenings a week back in the 80s. Lucky for Audrey.

Thrice weekly they met. Thrice weekly Terry Wogan made Blarney Stone–inspired, verbally dextrous love to Audrey. She in turn would giggle coquettishly at his smooth, knowing witticisms.

Terry Wogan flirted outrageously with Audrey! At least, that's how Audrey saw it. But there's a flipside to everything.

I noticed that she'd scowl jealously at any female guests. But more than that, Audrey would insist the other patients leave the room during her "private" and "intimate" time with her lover.

"Give us some privacy, *please*! This is our special time! My God, what are you? A bunch of voyeurs! Get out of here you perverts!"

It seemed Audrey had history.

Real consequences

In her youth, Audrey had been similarly in love with the actor David Niven, to the extent she spent all her time writing the mustachioed urbane actor love letters. He had once been her sole focus. And I do mean sole focus.

She'd had no time for her children, who were taken into care, or her husband, who had left her.

This is all a bit extreme, you might be thinking.

But while I was in that psychiatric hospital I learned an important lesson. I found that no one's psychological state was all that different from the rest of us. Extreme, yes, but not totally removed. All psychological states are merely different stages on *one continuum of human experience.*

We are all psychotic when we dream at night. And we all have fantasies. But some of us gather these fantasies from the deepest parts of our minds and place them firmly on the outside. And all emotional states and fantasies link back to the same human emotional needs.

However extreme some of the examples of needs gone awry may seem, hopefully you will recognize echoes of what I describe within your day-to-day life and client load.

One thing's for sure, we shouldn't underestimate the need for intimacy. It can determine the fate of our whole lives.

The need to be needed

Audrey needed to love and feel loved: "I'm so good for Terry!" she would tell me happily, "and he's so good for me!" Her *need* wasn't psychotic, just the way it was being expressed.

Her erstwhile husband had been cold, bullying, and "as distant as the planet Neptune, that you barely knew was there" as Audrey poetically put it. But there was real sadness in her poetry.

In this book on the dark side of human needs I explore how all human emotional difficulties stem from chronically *failing* to meet one or more of the primal emotional needs. It's absolutely critical that we know the causes of emotional problems.

But we're going further than that.

First know yourself

When we have a need, any need, we are compelled to meet it – often unconsciously.

Unless we can observe ourselves, this can cause confusion. We might think we are passionately promoting a cause or helping a friend when in fact we are instinctively trying to glean attention or some other basic need for ourselves. And there's nothing wrong with that... unless the *real* emotional drive starts to pollute the actual endeavour.

When we meet our needs in balance then we have spare capacity to do other things. The chronically hungry man is in no state to learn calculus. He may *think* he's learning, but in reality he's probably fumbling through student lockers looking for scraps of food and doing little else.

He needs to eat *outside* of the calculus lesson so he has the spare capacity to focus on his learning and let others learn too.

The analogy I've been using across this book is of extreme thirst driving us to drink *any* liquid, even engine oil. Desperation leads to terrible errors in whom we choose to be with and what kind of relationships we get involved in.

If we are *desperate* to meet a need, maybe even one we're unaware of, we are not just rendered less effective – we are also easy prey for dysfunctional, unscrupulous, or damaged others.

In the case of the need for intimacy, 'drinking engine oil' may mean falling for anyone who promises us intimacy. And that anyone might turn out to be really bad for us.

Love, love, love is a dangerous drug

All you need is love... right?

How about food, shelter, clothing, and, well, *all the other needs in balance*? Yes, they're pretty important too, but I don't want to rain on anyone's hippy parade. Love, real love, may be the essence of all and everything. But first things first.

I already wrote about the technique and dangers of 'love bombing'. For those who feel unloved, being showered with love can be overwhelming. And when the love turns out not to be real, payback may be more than anyone can afford.

If we understand the drive for intimacy, we can see how it can cause our clients terrible problems. We know that good relationships matter when it comes to health and happiness.[1]

Audrey had only ever received coldness from her abusive parents and ex-husband. Had she been truly loved and able to love, would her need for intimacy still have built up, grown, and flowered into full-blown psychotic delusion?

Here I want to simply describe how the need for intimacy can go awry. The consequences of 'toxic love', if you like. Let me give you a few examples.

Beware of transference

Sigmund Freud, you know, the expert on sex and... err... sex, and Greek myths, and sex, and cigars, and sex, and cocaine, and sex, was also very big on transference.

Freud said that a patient might feel attraction, even love, towards an analyst if they were never able to love their father, mother, or other parental figure in their childhood. It's possible to transfer negative feelings from one person to another. Of course it is. You're angry with your father, so you unconsciously redirect that to your therapist.

Mutual hate and hostility can form a kind of intimacy. In fact, some of the most intense relationships are ones of hate. The focus is mutual and fierce.

I think any therapy carries the danger of intimate feelings forming, especially if it is drawn out over many years or decades (as psychoanalysis tended to be). If you share your deepest desires and secrets with someone for many years, it's not surprising they might become vitally important to you.

There are even cases of therapists finding it hard to let go of patients! In the therapeutic setting intimacy can easily become entangled with the desire to help, and when this happens the 'therapy' can become lost... although Freudians might argue against that statement and assume transference is necessary.

Next we have a bizarre expression of intimacy that I think illuminates several aspects of human nature.

Stockholm syndrome: Loving the hands that bind

It can take many attempts for an abused person to actually leave their abuser. The victim's pattern of going back to the person who mistreats them can exasperate and shred the sympathy of friends and family.

Identifying with, even loving, the very source of abuse can seem baffling to those outside the relationship. How can they keep going back?

Intimacy, or the illusion of intimacy, can be produced through a sense of intensity which makes any relationship seem special.

We focus strongly on the people we feel intense with. That intensity can just as easily be brought about through fear and violence as through real love. And it often alternates with cherished nuggets of apparent kindness, which are appreciated all the more because of their rarity. "He can be so lovely!" ("And I am so, so grateful because it hardly ever happens!")

So why 'Stockholm'?

In 1973 in Stockholm, Swedish robbers took bank workers hostage, locked them in a back safe, and threatened them with death. They were held hostage for days and nights on end.

But, bafflingly, when authorities moved in to end the siege some of the kidnapped bank workers resisted rescue. Some refused to testify against their captors despite having been treated terribly.

As a result, the phenomenon of identifying with or loving the person causing you harm came to be known as Stockholm syndrome.

I've previously written about how Stockholm syndrome might even be an element of smoking and other addictions. We can see addiction as a kind of abusive relationship which nevertheless feels intimate and therefore hard to let go.

When thinking about intimacy it's important to remember that we focus on what *is* important to us, but it also works the other way. What we focus on *becomes* important to us. Take the Florence Nightingale effect.

I'm caring for you, so I must care about you!

Ever read or seen Stephen King's *Misery*? It's great! Author Paul Sheldon's creepy "number one fan" Annie Wilkes finds him after a serious car crash and, rather than taking the poor guy to hospital, she drags him to her house to nurse him back to health without telling a soul (well, spoiler alert, at one point she takes a sledgehammer to his leg – but otherwise her nursing is pretty A-grade).

Okay, so Ms Wilkes was obviously pretty obsessed already, but now she is focused on her 'patient' *all* the time. And for his part, she's the only person he can rely on. The relationship has become intimate for them both in different ways.

The Florence Nightingale effect can come about when a caregiver (not necessarily an actual nurse as our Florence was) develops intense feelings for the person she or he is caring for. This can happen even if there isn't much actual communication or contact between the two.

This might seem like a pretty rare situation. But I think it can work in another way.

I've seen looks of terror flood partners' faces when they realize I might actually be able to help their loved one lose weight, overcome agoraphobia, or otherwise reclaim their rightful independence. The 'carer' may fear, perhaps unconsciously, that they will lose intimacy if the balance of power changes and they are no longer needed in the same capacity.

If you fear someone will need you less, you might also fear they will *want* you less. It's worth bearing this in mind as a potential mechanism in some of our clients' situations.

But perhaps a bit more familiar is the scary phenomenon of stalking.

"I never knew when he would just turn up!"

Sally, a client, told me how her ex-boyfriend still stalked her. The terror was in the unpredictability. He would "just show up" at her work, her home, even when she was out with friends and it seemed as if there was no way he could possibly have known her whereabouts.

For both men and women, stalking often reflects an inability or refusal to accept the end of intimacy. But sometimes it stems from the illusion of intimacy or a misjudged attempt at initiating intimacy.

"We're meant to be together! Why can't you admit that too?"

Becoming infatuated is not uncommon at all. But becoming so hooked that you can think about *nothing else*, even (or especially) if you don't really know the person beyond the fantasy you've created in your head, is a real problem. This is a poor substitute for genuine love, intimacy, and mutual understanding.

Assuming someone just doesn't realize they love you yet is a dangerous perception. To try to force intimacy, or to imagine it's there when it isn't, is to chase false gold.

Ultimately we need to be strong enough to be alone if we have to be.

How safe are you?

When we really love someone, we run the risk of 'putting all our eggs in one basket'. But if I *only* want to be with you, what happens if you decide you *never* want to be with me?

When our clients are intensely afraid of rejection, over-monitor their lover, or feel they couldn't exist without them, we need to look at how many of their needs are met through just this one person.

To be less vulnerable, we need to meet our needs *in balance* – to avoid putting all our eggs in one basket. When a person enters a relationship and stops seeing their other friends or pursuing other interests, this makes them vulnerable. If I only eat one type of food and that disappears, I might feel I can't survive.

On the other hand, having a healthy wider life, other friends, and other interests makes us less desperate, less vulnerable, and less devastated if it doesn't work out.

So we may need to encourage a reconnection with wider friends and family to, in a sense, dilute the power that 'special' person has over them. No break-up is easy, but the more *wider support* a person has the easier it will be.

On the more sinister side, if a person *wants* you to become overly dependent on them they will actively seek to distance you from other sources of focus, such as your friends, family, and wider interests. Cults do this too.

If someone knows you are solely wrapped up in them, they know they have the power to manipulate, threaten, and abuse you – "Without me you're nothing!"

Yes, the drive for intimacy is strong, and yes, it can lead down all kinds of prickly paths. And sometimes it can be a complete fabrication.

When they don't even know who you are

We can easily come to feel we are intimate with a leader or celebrity. We see their face and hear their voice so often that they *seem* such a part of our lives.

Joseph Stalin, the mass murdering leader of Soviet Russia, was known as 'Uncle Joe'. At first the nickname was just used by Churchill and Roosevelt, but he came to be *generally* known by this moniker.

The genocidal tyrant of Haiti, François Duvalier, was known sweetly as 'Papa Doc'. And of course it was 'Big Brother' who was watching you in Orwell's dystopian nightmare.

Uncle, Papa, Brother!

The illusion of intimacy, the dim and twisted cousin of real intimacy, is everywhere. But we can't settle. We need to seek the real thing, because it *is* there.

The real gold of intimacy may be *discovered* on the internet but, to be actualized, it has to travel through that looking glass of pixels into the real world.

So many of us seem to live alone in our isolated heads, but if we're lucky, we might find a secret door to a connecting bridge where we can meet and merge with that special friend or lover.

CHAPTER FIVE
CONNECTION

HOW THE NEED FOR COMMUNITY AND CONNECTION CAN LEAD TO DISTRESS, CRUELTY, AND SELF-DESTRUCTION

> *"We are like islands in the sea, separate on the surface but connected in the deep."*
>
> WILLIAM JAMES

> *"In crowds it is stupidity and not mother wit that is accumulated."*
>
> GUSTAVE LE BON

Fascism! What an emotive word! It's a word that has become synonymous with violence, hate, racism, and persecution. But the term wasn't always an insult. Indeed, in the early days of Italian fascism it was President Franklin D. Roosevelt who said:

> *"I am much interested and deeply impressed by what he [Mussolini] has accomplished and by his evidenced honest purpose of restoring Italy".*

The word 'fascism' comes from the Roman *fasces*, meaning a bundle of sticks that may be weak individually but become strong when bound tightly together.

While Mussolini didn't initially seem interested in persecuting people because of their race like Hitler did (in fact, he saw racism as ridiculous)[1], he was certainly all for violence and war if it meant promoting Italian nationalism. Mussolini felt that the collective should always take precedence over the individual:

> "Everything in the state, nothing outside the state, nothing against the state."
>
> BENITO MUSSOLINI

The people were there to serve the state, not the other way around. Individualism? Forget it. Centralized state control was everything. Fall away from the bundle of sticks and you might just be snapped in half. But if some sticks happen to break, well, never mind. They were weak anyway!

It's easy to feel superior to past peoples who were bamboozled by a monomaniacal leader. But the drive for conformity and group identity is powerful. And anything powerful can be dangerous.

It's also easy to assume that a client's problems happen in a vacuum. But we are merged in groups. And groups can start to act like mass personalities in their own right.

It's always worth asking ourselves, especially if a client identifies strongly with some group or other: What are the beliefs, ideals, and assumptions of the group? Is the *group* identity dysfunctional in any way?

Your decisions? Or your tribe's?

Mussolini, Hitler, Stalin, Jim Jones... any cult leader, in fact *any* leader, appeals to our innate instinct to merge with a greater group, be it a national or a political identity. "Stronger together!" Bundled sticks.

As with all the basic emotional needs, some people have a greater drive to merge as part of a group than others. Ironically, the true individualists, the 'lone wolves', may be the very ones at the top of the heap, getting everyone *else* to merge.

"Join us! Twenty million people can't be wrong!"

Some leaders are more benign than others of course. But they have one defining feature in common: they play on our innate human need for connection to something bigger than ourselves, to a *tribe*.

People may come to identify themselves through their tribe first and foremost. This sounds noble, even selfless, but it can have grave consequences. If everyone is doing it, you'll do it too. But what if 'it' is very bad indeed?

We need to understand how desire for group membership and groupthink works, because it can and often *does* work against us.

Taking poison instead of medicine

In this book I explore the dark side of our innate human needs, how an emotional need can become so intense that we seek to meet it from *anywhere*.

If we are dying of dehydration it may *seem* like a good idea to drink engine oil – it's a liquid, isn't it? But to do so puts our very lives at risk.

Lonely people may be more likely to get sucked in by manipulative con artists or narcissists. After all, what is loneliness if not a 'thirst' for connection, intimacy, and attention? They may become so 'thirsty', the need may become so great, that they drink poison instead of water.

When we meet our needs in balance we have *spare capacity* to be effective and fulfilled. When our life provides us with emotional fulfilment, we become less vulnerable to being manipulated, led by the nose, ushered to the cliff's edge.

I think the entire human race needs to understand how this works. Urgently. It may be getting too late for us *not* to absorb the available information as to how we are all manipulated by our innate needs.

A drive to meet an emotional need isn't good or bad. It just *is*. But any drive can be railroaded or diverted, and *that's* the problem. We may be tempted to hand over autonomy to anyone who seems to meet our needs for meaning, togetherness, self-esteem, or whatever it is we are lacking.

Mind you, some level of drive for group togetherness is inherently healthy. It has and does keep us alive.

Stay or die!

You may be smarter than a lion, but you don't bite as hard, rip as fiercely or move as powerfully.

As human beings developed, we had to evolve *collectively*, to form tribes. We were stronger in groups than individually. Safety in numbers protected us against predators and maintained our position in the natural dominance hierarchy. Organizing ourselves, socializing, made us strong and able to survive and thrive.

On the flipside, to leave or be cast out from the tribe meant almost certain death. And for many people, that is still a primal fear.

Recent research has found that being ostracized by co-workers or a social group, what some call the 'social death penalty', is more injurious than being overtly bullied.[2] It seems that no attention or connection is worse than negative attention. Rejection registers in the brain in almost exactly the same way as *physical* pain.[3]

On the positive side, being accepted and actively participating in a wider social network, a 'tribe', confers huge psychological and physical benefits.[4]

Feeling mutually supported is wonderful. It sure must have felt wonderful for early members of the Nazi Party! The power of being part of the in-group. The feeling of being special, mutually supported, respected, even feared simply for being in your tribe. Feeling you suddenly have a respected identity can feel amazing.

We can simply judge people as evil. But that is superficial, because *most* people are not evil. They've just fallen into the trap of following those who are.

Research shows that being in a group can make people lose touch with their moral code.[5] This is sometimes called 'mob mentality'. We can get swept up in a kinetic and sweeping wave of self-righteous rage that floods the whole group. Sometimes it's not until years later that we even think to question what happened: "How did I *act* like that?" Sometimes we never reach that realization.

The first step towards understanding the power of the group over individual mentality is, I think, not to assume it's only *other* people who could suffer from groupthink or 'group*feel*'. We are all susceptible at some level.

Ultimately we all have to answer to ourselves, whether we act as part of a group or not.

We all need to feel a sense of community, a feeling that we are making a contribution to a cause beyond and greater than ourselves. This is a legitimate need and is often positive.

And any situation that helps us focus less *just on the self* tends to make us feel better because our life takes on *meaning*. Ultimately it never feels meaningful just to focus on one's own concerns. And when life feels meaningful, we feel motivated and therefore happier.

But just because we have a real need doesn't mean we should hand over our rationality and individual judgement.

10 simple steps to dangerous conformity

Here they are: ten ways in which the drive for social connection can backfire when we try to meet it indiscriminately. You may recognize in them some of your own experiences, and those of friends, relatives or clients.

1. Lack purpose, social connection and meaning

People looking for purpose, safety, and status may be more likely to follow any group that promises to meet these needs. The more disconnected and purposeless the person feels, the more susceptible they become.

The price of entry? The unsavoury belief system of the group's leaders.

If you're lonely and everyone else seems to be taking drugs, then taking drugs may seem a small price to pay to enter the social network. The temptation isn't the drugs themselves, or even the excitement or criminality. It's the sense of community, of doing what others are doing.

Most people will not recognize they have joined a group because of their innate needs. They may assume it's the ideals of the group that attracted them. Indeed, it's worth remembering that all group ideologies involve feeling morally right. The bad guys always *think* they're the good guys.

2. Conform at all costs

The need to conform is, for many people, irresistibly strong. And it can build steadily.

Peer pressure feels like pressure even if it's not stated overtly. People give in to peer pressure because that's the price you pay to be a member of the tribe. They do it because everyone else is, or because the leader or other members of the group demand it (or even just imply it). This short clip (https://www.youtube.com/watch?v=TYIh4MkcfJA) shows how conformity can happen on a physical level even with no apparent pressure.

Sally, a young client, told me how, as a child, she had joined in with bullying her former best friend at school. The girl had later committed suicide. "Everyone else was doing it and I just went along with it!" she told me, shamefaced.

Conformity of language, ideas, and dress are all signs that someone is handing over their personal identity to a group. But it's not just what we do on the outside that counts.

3. Put the group's aims above your own moral code

We all know that some people are prepared to die for the 'greater good' (which may actually be bad) of the group. This kind of self-destruction may take many forms. Perhaps a suicide vest, or a one-way kamikaze flight. But it's not always so obvious.

Some people may feel so connected to, say, a group of

drinkers, drug takers, or dangerous thrill seekers that in some sense the group becomes all-important to them. Loyalty to a counterculture that holds you back may maintain dysfunctionality or misery. It may even kill you.

A drug overdose or accident may happen because the person felt they *couldn't* survive beyond or outside of the group. Yes, the drugs killed them, but maybe their forged identity as a 'drug addict' or 'drinker' was really to blame.

When we ask a drug addict to stop taking drugs, we may also be asking them to forgo their whole community or even sense of purpose. The 'addiction' may be to the group or lifestyle as much as the substance. And unless the needs this group fulfils can be met healthily elsewhere, any therapy is bound to fail.

4. Let the group manipulate you using shame, threats, and promises

In order to indoctrinate, group dynamics must be highly emotional, both in language and in behaviour. Interrelational emotions, such as shame (public shaming or 'outing'), embarrassment, and rivalry are ramped up to the max in order to keep the focus on group identity.

Hope for advancement within the group, the promise of reward or an increase in status, easily transforms into fear of loss of status, of being cast out. Continual alternation between fear and hope is what sustains the vicious cycle of groupthink.

The next step might be the most horrible of all.

5. Denigrate outsiders

To strengthen group identity there needs to be an enemy,

real or imagined. On no account can outsiders be seen as being in any way like you.

The enemy is simplistically seen as 'bad'. This process of denigrating outsiders strengthens group identity, gives the group purpose, and prevents dissent. Ideas that are not part of the group's ideological lexicon or dogma are not tolerated.

Opposing groups or individuals are labelled as 'bad', 'mad', 'stupid', or simply 'misguided'. They are regularly blamed, shamed, belittled, and, in some cases, dehumanized. Dehumanizing and therefore objectifying outsiders is the first step towards justified violence.

The Nazis described and depicted Jews as 'rats'. In the Rwandan genocide of between half and one million Tutsis in 100 days, the Tutsis were repeatedly described as 'cockroaches'. When you liken the enemy to vermin, it's not hard to convince people they should be exterminated.

Rats, cockroaches, squares, commies, fascists, unbelievers! The list goes on. Outsiders may become no more than one-dimensional objects. And once the out-group is objectified, violence can swiftly follow – because objects can be disposed of.

We can have loose affiliations to many groups, but the more power a group has over an individual's life the more they'll start to fall into a repetitive pattern.

6. Partake of frequent, ritualistic, repetitive activities

Ritual, repetition, and provocation of collective emotion are all indoctrination techniques.[6] Any group, even one professing to be atheist, can behave like a religion in the way it organizes its activities and engineers the belief of its adherents.

Again, some groups that do this have a positive effect on

people and communities. Belief engineering through ritual occurs in all types of strong groups.

7. Blindly defer to authority

For some people, leaders may come to replace a father or a mother. This can confer a warm sense of security. After all, if everything is taken care of by someone who knows better than me, life becomes simple. Just like when I was little!

American social scientist Stanley Milgram showed that ordinary people are often prompted to do horrible things simply because they are told it's okay, or even desirable, by an authority figure.[7] If Mummy or Daddy says it's okay, then it must be! (Just as "if everyone else is doing it, it must be okay for me to do it too!")

8. Use not just groupthink, but also groupspeak

The 'f' word at the start of this piece is proof that words can carry great power.

Only individualists or leaders use original language (usually carefully curated to their advantage). Other members of the group are so strongly conditioned to follow that they will naturally adopt that same system of language.

The stronger a group identity, the more the same all its members sound when they communicate. Just talk like everyone else, and you'll be fine!

Enough said.

9. On no account try to understand outside perspectives

Ideally, subsist in your in-group echo chamber. Don't listen to dissenting, conflicting, or unorthodox ideas. In fact, actively shut down or otherwise drown out ideas which conflict with your group thought.

There is no reality beyond the group.

Finally...

10. Lose your mind in mob mentality

As the writer Gustave Le Bon observed in his seminal book *The Crowd: A Study of The Popular Mind*, individual intelligence and reasoning can be lost when caught up in a mob. The mob takes on a will of its own, like some kind of raving beast. Lenin, Mussolini, Freud, and Stalin were all fans of Le Bon's work.[8]

Belonging to a group can make us more prepared to do violence because the *mob wills it.*[9]

And now, for the sake of balance....

3 steps to resisting group mentality

1. Understand how it works. Without an understanding of how group psychology works humanity is condemned to make the same mistakes over and over.

2. Meet your needs for connection in healthy ways. Ways that don't damage you or others. This will give you *spare capacity.* You won't be so 'thirsty' that you end up drinking whatever's on offer.

3. Maintain objectivity. Stay calm and use your psychological knowledge. Recognize what is really going on above and beyond slogans, propaganda, whipped-up emotionality, and the 'us and them' mentality.

The need to connect to larger groups is powerful and inherent. Understanding how group psychology works frees us up to *see it operating in everyday life*, within ourselves and others.

Seeing the part that group psychology plays in the formation and maintenance of emotional and behavioural problems is vital in order to protect ourselves, collectively (as in the whole human race), from extinction.

Together we *are* stronger. But strength without compassion, fairness, calmness, and an understanding of human nature is worse than useless, as history has repeatedly shown. It's time we learned our lesson.

CHAPTER SIX
STATUS

HOW THE NEED FOR STATUS CAN LEAD TO BULLYING AND SELF-DESTRUCTION

"The world more often rewards outward signs of merit than merit itself."

FRANÇOIS DE LA ROCHEFOUCAULD

Riches. Strength. Height, slenderness, muscularity. Being the best at something. Being the *worst.* Being the funniest. The rudest. The most beautiful. The most intelligent. The most aggressive. The most notorious.

Being top dog, cat, gorilla, or official. Wearing the latest clothes or uniform. Owning the most land. Having the most attractive or dominant partner. A bigger house. The best vacations. Knowing the right people. Knowing the *most* people. Signaling the most virtue.

Status isn't about *being* these things. Status is about being *seen* to be or to have these things relative to others. But, like any legitimate human need, wanting to be *recognized* can easily morph from a need to a demanding, all-consuming greed.

Status is a constant in human life. Though much of the time we don't think about it because it's everywhere and takes so many forms.

So why is the drive for status so strong?

The universal need for recognition and control

We all need some sense of control to avoid feeling helpless and hopeless. You see it in infants striving for independence. One of my own earliest memories (I think it's a real one!) was of feeling outraged at being stuck in my cot and managing to climb out. The drive to walk, feed oneself, and talk are all about gaining more control.

The need for recognition, attention, and esteem merge into what we call 'status'.

When we feel recognized, appreciated, and respected, we have more control. We have status. And feeling valued and admired for who or what we are can meet the need for attention and personal power in spades.

Status is a kind of frozen, focused, sustainable way of eliciting attention from people. And high status, wide recognition, helps us live longer and healthier lives.

Actors and directors who win Oscars live longer than those merely nominated.[1] The thought of seeking status for its own sake has distasteful connotations for many. But *lack* of status can cause real problems, including dying younger and having worse mental and physical health outcomes.[2,3]

Being at the bottom of the pile, low in the 'pecking order', or, perhaps worse, suffering a *loss* of status, seems toxic not just for humans but for other animals too.[4]

Conversely, feeling appreciated can help foster healthy self-esteem. We like to feel esteemed for what we are and can do. In this way social status, being and feeling recognized for our position, whether it be manager, worker, mother, or good friend, helps us feel our place in the world.

But many clients suffer because they feel *unappreciated*, or 'invisible'.

So the higher the position in a hierarchy we occupy, the greater health, self-esteem, happiness, and longevity we enjoy. Status matters, but if status is abused or becomes all-consuming, it turns into a pernicious poison.

We feel envy when we dislike the fact that someone has or is something we would like to have or be. Envy is essentially resentment of another's status. And advertisers know this.

Status updates

"Be the envy of your friends!" is a perennial advertising message. But why would you want your friends to suffer envy?

Much of human behaviour consists of instinctive or conscious attempts to gain higher status. We fight, some of us more than others, to rise in the dominance hierarchy, in whatever form it may take.

In this book I explore the dark side of what are, in balance, *healthy* and vital emotional needs. We all need to drink water, and we should do so when we need it. But drinking engine oil, or even too much water, can kill us.

There are, of course, different kinds of status. Conspicuously displaying wealth is the most obvious kind, but hierarchies come in many different flavours. Even the sentiment "status doesn't matter to me!" (i.e. "I'm *above* status!") may be a status signal.

But one thing's for sure: The *drive* for status, while inherent and instinctive (no matter what we might tell ourselves!) can lead us to some dark places.

"I don't know who I'm supposed to be!"

One risk of focusing solely on status is that we can lose ourselves in the process.

Take my client Geoff. Geoff was driven. He always had been. "Second is first loser!" That's what he told me his dad used to tell him when he was at school.

Geoff's whole life had been a struggle to be the best. "Not the best *I* can be, but the best *anybody* can be!"

Geoff had come to see me because he'd hit another patch of depression. A signal from his deep self that his life wasn't working the way he was living it. His workaholism was destroying him and his marriage.

He was successful, financially secure, and well respected and known in his field. But he felt the whipcrack of his emotional conditioning every moment of every day.

"I'm not being arrogant, but people see me as the best at what I do. But... I don't know who I *am* anymore. I don't know who I'm *supposed* to be! I don't do anything unless it somehow ties in with getting better, rising up to be the best!"

Since the depression had hit, however, he'd found himself unable to do much of anything. So what was the problem?

If we focus entirely on our status, on rising and maintaining our position in our chosen dominance hierarchy, then status becomes the main object of our lives. *Extrinsic* reward replaces *intrinsic* reward. And the more that happens, the less meaningful our lives can feel. Why? Because only *intrinsic* reward makes your life feel meaningful.

Why exactly do you do what you do?

Back in 1973, psychologists Mark R. Lepper and David Greene found that rewarding children with praise and attention for doing an activity which they *had been enjoying for its own sake* had the effect of lessening the child's interest and motivation in that activity.[5]

Being rewarded with attention and praise, or being told you are good, eats away at motivation – because the activity no longer provides intrinsic reward, but rather extrinsic reward.

Geoff had come to feel that something was only worth doing if it in somehow reflected or increased his status. The idea of *inherently* or intrinsically enjoying an activity for its own sake had all but vanished for him.

Another client would spend money she didn't have just to enhance her perceived status. She would spend all her hard-earned cash – and then some – on lavish haute-couture clothes, a fancy car, and eye-wateringly expensive jewellery. All just "to impress people". She was tens of thousands of pounds in debt by the time she came to me for help.

When we treat clients, we can try to ascertain how much of their life is predicated on how they imagine others see them and how they *want* to be seen. Sure, *some* proportion of our efforts can be linked to status, and that needn't be a problem. But what proportion?

If we just want to be 'the best' (at the top of a chosen hierarchy), we may become *less* motivated than, say, if 85% of our motivation is for love of, or belief in, the activity itself.

A key question, then, is how much of what we do is linked to how we *seem* to others?

When we forget the difference between who we are and who we seem *in comparison* to others, we are walking the road to unhappiness. We are losing all sense of meaning in life. We are losing *ourselves*.

But what about the dangerous side of *getting* more status? Because, for some, increased status is the last thing they need.

The Killing Tree

I was in Cambodia visiting one of the 'killing fields', and before us stood a single tree. Our guide bravely fought back tears as she told us her father had vanished during those nightmarish times. Her smiling face showed flashes of agony as she pointed out the strands of human hair still ingrained in the bark. This was the Killing Tree.

Not wanting to waste bullets, the communist regime Khmer Rouge would swing children against the tree to kill them. Teeth still washed up in the earth when it rained.

I asked the guide who had sanctioned this barbarity. She said:

"The one at the top. Him. Pol Pot." Of course, he hadn't actually done it himself. But he *had* given the orders to the men and women who had been appointed with the status to do it.

A kind of madness can descend on someone when they are granted a dramatic increase in status.

It's easy to blithely assume that if *we* were in power the world would sing in harmony and be bathed in eternal sunshine. But infinite arrogance aside, it does seem that being given authority, the status of official or custodian of power, is toxic for many. We shouldn't assume it wouldn't be toxic for us, too.

In fact, to believe *we* could handle a great increase in power simply because we assume we are not prey to the dark forces of human nature is to take the first fateful step *towards* tyranny.

People have done terrible things because of newly conferred status. People who, *despite their best intentions*, find that power really does corrupt. And this corruption can happen at lightning speed.

Sadistic students

Status can easily go to our heads and make us cruel and tyrannical. For some people, all it takes is a uniform for them to lose themselves to monstrous cruelty.

Back in 1971, Stanford's Professor Philip Zimbardo conducted the infamous 'prison experiment'.[6] He wanted to study and observe the effects of perceived power, focusing on the behavioural and emotional interplay between prisoners and prison officers.

Interestingly, the study was financed by the US Office of Naval Research as an investigation into the causes of difficulties between guards and prisoners in the US Navy and US Marine Corps.

College students were *randomly* assigned the role of prisoner or guard. The effects of this status assignation were immediate and shocking.

People were free to leave the experiment any time they wanted, but many prisoners very soon fell into a passive role, accepting any and all treatment they received.

Psychological torture of the prisoners by the guards was so quick to assert itself that it took only six days before Zimbardo's future wife urged him to stop the experiment. Bear in mind that these were liberal-minded students who may well have denied *they* would ever be intoxicated by power.

It was concluded that it wasn't the students' inherent personality attributes that caused their behaviour, but the *situation itself*. The status they had been given. Oh, and if you're interested, here's a slightly disturbing trailer for a movie made about the Stanford Prison Experiment.

We all have a need for control, and the more status we feel, the more power we feel – and that equates to a sense of control.

But feeling more control over *yourself* could easily tip into a desire to extend that sense of control by controlling *me* (and vice versa). This is how tyrannies become established. And I don't just mean the great big obvious Orwellian tyrannies. I mean those petty social-circle bullying ones too.

It's easy to focus on the sadism of the students assigned high status in this study, but I'm also interested in the way most of the 'prisoners' sank into passivity.

It's important to understand that 'victim' is also a status.

Victimhood status

When we label someone, we assign them a status.

When you have a sense of status (whether high or low), you feel that certain behaviours are expected of you. If we assign someone the role of 'victim', that is, a low position in the hierarchy, they may come – as the 'prisoners' did in the Stanford experiment – to feel, and ultimately *be* passive.

We can see a client's sense of status by just talking and listening to them. How much influence do they feel in their life over themselves and others?

A victim is, by definition, *not a victor* over events or circumstances. To describe someone as a victim is to ascribe them low status if the label becomes permanently stuck.

Support groups can be valuable in that people feel they are not alone with a condition or in their feelings, but ultimately 'victim' isn't a status that serves anyone well for long.

Paradoxically, sometimes the low status of 'victim', if victimhood itself is respected or encouraged, can place a person quite *high* in the status hierarchy. This is a problem when it becomes aspirational to be seen as a victim, consciously or otherwise.

But status can also be gleaned by or entangled with who you know, and this has its own dangers.

Jailhouse love

Notoriety is, of course, a form of high status. Alpha can take many forms.

I want to talk about a phenomenon which, while relatively rare, is still common *enough* to tell us something important about the attraction of status and how we can bask in other people's.

A killer behind bars is notorious. Therefore he has high status and *some* women will find that intriguing or downright attractive (though men don't seem to so commonly fall for female incarcerated killers).[7]

We can gain status by 'being with' high-status people. Of course, if someone is behind bars, the relationship isn't a full one – but the woman can still elicit some kind of reflected status by being romantically involved with a notorious, high-status male.

She may spout all the clichés about feeling she is the only one who really knows him, or can see the good in him, or can tame him, and so on and so forth, but ultimately she has chosen a high-status male (as weird as that sounds).

More prosaically, if you ever wonder, "What on earth he or she could possibly see in them!?" it might just be their status: their level of social or other dominance. Hanging out with the 'cool' naughty kid at school can, in the same way, confer status.

It's a mistake, I think, to assume status doesn't matter, that we are above it, or that it *shouldn't* matter. Quite clearly it does – in all kinds of ways.

Once we learn to recognize the role of status in all kinds of human behaviours, motivation becomes easier to read. And understanding status can, of course, help us understand abuses of power.

Ideas to prop up status

Fighting toxic ideologies is all very well, but it misses a vital point.

Warped status can lead to tyranny, yes, but tyranny isn't about ideology. Ideas are simply the floating bubbles in the seething molten seas of emotion. They are the rationale and sometimes the excuse for power plays. They simply prop up the status of controlling, tyrannical people.

And when status becomes more important than substance, we are in trouble. *Seeming* to be 'the expert' may replace *actual* expertise or competence.

Status can be derived in all kinds of ways, from victimhood, to having more stuff (which equates to power), to looking better, being smarter, knowing more gossip, or being the most popular.

The point here is none of these characteristics *have* to be connected to status unless that's the way these attributes are seen by others or (instinctively) felt by the person.

Some people use their *official* status to bully and intimidate. They can't even psychologically handle the uniform of a petty official without becoming tyrannical. Others base their whole sense of self on being some kind of official, a 'successful' businessperson, or some other status, and ram it down everyone's throats at any opportunity.

But there is a universal corrective to overly rigid dominance hierarchies.

Laugh and the whole world gets annoyed

Some people may choose jobs that automatically confer status and authority. And we have to hope they can manage that power. But I think it's important to be able to relax with a sense of status. To *always* have to keep our dignity, to *always* have to seem serious or capable, paradoxically lowers our real power.

There is a kind of transcendence at being able to laugh at ourselves or those of high status. Tyrannies don't like humour. They may even try to control the content of jokes because it threatens their status as total purveyors of reality. Only *certain* jokes are okay.

Having humour about status, not having to take ourselves or others too seriously, is a great counterbalance to the loss of perspective status can inflict.

The need for status (including online popularity, approval, and attention) can stop us living our life from our *own* perspective. When we go down the rabbit hole of "How does this make me *seem*?" rather than "What do *I* think about this?" we have already begun to lose who we really are.

Ultimately, status doesn't necessarily equate to wisdom, intelligence, judiciousness, or decency. And yet we might have been conditioned to defer to it unquestionably.

Being automatically anti-authoritarian might be a way of trying to raise our own status, but we shouldn't be automatically pro-authority either. Not blindly so.

In the words of Paulo Coelho, "What other people think of you is none of your business!"

CHAPTER SEVEN
CHALLENGE

HOW THE DIVERTED NEED FOR CHALLENGE WRECKS LIVES

"A wild longing for strong emotions and sensations seethes in me, a rage against this toneless, flat, normal and sterile life. I have a mad impulse to smash something, a warehouse, perhaps, or a cathedral, or myself, to commit outrages, to pull off the wigs of a few revered idols..."

FROM *STEPPENWOLF*, BY HERMANN HESSE

When have you felt most alive? I'm willing to bet it's when you've been so engrossed, so engaged in some part of life that nothing else mattered in the moment. Perhaps you were rising to some sublime creative challenge or surmounting some difficulty you had no idea you could surmount.

How do we *feel* in such times?

The self, with all its complications, preoccupations, and procrastination, is suspended as you become pure awareness and action in times like this.

Being frequently engaged and fascinated makes us feel alive. But the opposite to this is a kind of deadness of the soul.

Many of us are bored.

Boredom, before we know it, will break us. A *lack* of challenge and excitement leads to a sense that life is meaningless. As long as there is no or little challenge or surprise we disengage, become depressed, no longer feel alive.

"The Devil makes work for idle hands" – and unstimulated minds.

Without meaning we feel stale and lost. We are here to learn, flourish, work toward our potentials (we have many). We need to feel activated, intrigued, invigorated and enlivened by our days, at least some of the time.

In this book I look at what we need as human beings to be happy and healthy. The 'human givens' of what it means to exist in our world. I've already looked at, among other needs, how a need for attention – a vital and totally legitimate need – can be subverted to cause us, and others, harm.

I return to the same analogy I've been pushing throughout the book: You need water, but if your need is *too* great or if you have never learned to distinguish water from engine oil, then you may 'drink' what is poisonous to you. We do this when we instinctively seek to fulfil emotional needs in ways that backfire.

Understanding how this happens helps us to see why human beings, both individually and collectively, develop and cause problems.

So what about our universal need for creativity and challenge? Well, the first thing to understand is that it varies from person to person. Mine and yours may be really different.

Are you a high or low gainer?

Positron emission tomography (try keeping your false teeth in when you say that!), or PET scans, have found that sensation-seeking extroverts have lower levels of arousal in a particular area of their brainstems than more withdrawn, less sensation-seeking introverts.[1]

The reticular activating system (RAS) is tuned differently in low gainers (extroverts) versus high gainers (introverts). If your RAS is tuned low, you will get bored easily and seek excitement and sensation because not much is going on inside.

But if there is a higher level of RAS arousal in your brainstem, you'll seek to keep things quiet and calm *on the outside.* You will want to avoid too much external stimulation because there is more than enough happening *inside* you.

So some people *need* more external challenge than others. It's important to understand this within our clients too. We all have *some* need for creative challenge and excitement, but the intensity of this need, like any need, varies from person to person. Some people have more of the openness trait and are naturally more attuned to seeking out novelty and challenge.

But whether we're naturally a high gainer or a low gainer, we all need *enough* creative challenge. And when we don't have enough, we suffer – and sometimes *other people* suffer too.

Boredom brings with it many problems, but is also *symptomatic.*

Does overstimulation lead to boredom?

Notwithstanding all the benefits (and there are many) of electronic information access and connectivity, it may be that all the current weapons of mass distraction and immediacy, social media and all that, may be training our brains to lose the capacity for prolonged and deep focus.[2]

When focused fully, the mind can be absorbed and stimulated enough by something as simple as a sunset.

But when it can't help but flit about like an intoxicated blue-bottomed fly from one update to the next, the mind can be bored even amid plenty of stimulation.

The boredom comes from within, because, although there is stimulation from without, there is no real *meaning* being generated. Attention isn't being *extended* and fixed toward anything productive. It just slides around aimlessly, like an untethered lifeboat in a storm.

Never have we had so much access to experience, information, and each other. Yet somehow boredom seems to be *increasing* – especially in the young.[3]

So what can a *lack* of meaningful creative challenge do to people?

The siren call of the unmet need

The stultifying sensation of boredom is a signal. A siren call. A seductive urge that calls you to...

- Have that affair!
- Gamble!
- Start a fight!
- Be needlessly outraged!
- Bully 'for kicks'!
- Take drugs!
- Drink yourself into bewilderment!

This is not to say that *all* these activities are necessarily or wholly *caused* by the unfulfilled need for challenge or excitement – but they *can* be.

There certainly appears to be a link between impulsivity (including gambling and other risk taking) and *proneness* to boredom.[4]

And if we have failed to observe what we are like we may never spot the pattern in ourselves. We may assume we (or our clients) gamble for 'deeper' reasons. That's why it's so important to know how our primal basic needs drive our behaviour: so that we can avoid destructive blindness when it comes to our own and our clients' actions.

Always ask: What emotional need might this action be *trying* to fulfil?

Rationalizing, justifying and lying to ourselves

Psychology didn't just develop to understand *other* people. When we assume we are doing something for one reason but really there is *another* reason driving our behaviour, we are in effect being tyrannized by our *own* psychology.

It's easier, and more flattering, to convince yourself you are attending that protest march because you really believe in the cause rather than because it meets (or seems to meet) an unmet need for excitement (and attention – I address this in some depth in Chapter One: The Dark Side of the Need for Attention).

If I am outraged or join a marauding mob essentially because I am bored in life, but I *believe* that I am doing the collective marauding for other reasons (after all, it takes some integrity and courage to look at ourselves squarely and to see our *real* motivations), then I am taking several large leaps *away* from self-knowledge.

The problem with being disconnected from our own motivations is that we cease to be productive and measured in the way we live our lives. We are led around by the nose, so to speak. We pursue anything that seems to meet an immediate emotional need, and avoid anything (even if it is vital) that *doesn't* seem to meet an immediate emotional need.

But if we can meet our needs for challenge, excitement and creative effort productively, then we don't need to blindly seek a destructive challenge (such as a fight) or seek out needless risk.

But there's more. When not properly challenged, the creative drive can cause us still *other* problems – some of which can tip us into depression.

Imagination: a tool for self-harm?

"I don't have the time to worry!" I heard a woman say recently. And it got me thinking. What is worry? Well, in essence, it's a use – often an *uncontrolled* use – of the imagination.

You need *creativity* to worry. And after seeing thousands of clients over the decades, believe me when I say that people can find incredibly creative ways of worrying. I've seen people create scary, depressing inner scenarios about stuff that I wouldn't even have had the *imagination* to worry about!

Yes, at the far end of the spectrum, the imagination can become so out of control, so intense, that people even hallucinate. We all do this during dream sleep or during extreme sensory deprivation. But those prone to psychosis may live within their uncontrollable created realities for extended periods.[5]

We can see psychosis, then, as extreme, out-of-control creativity.

But, short of psychosis, many of us do spend too much time focusing on what we *imagine*, sometimes to the point that the line between our imaginings and our actual observations of external reality becomes blurred. These imaginings can be extremely scary or depressing. And we know that worrying or negative rumination drives and maintains depression.[6]

We might imagine others don't like us or that we have done something wrong, or paint bleak futures and generally follow the dictates of our created inner constructs, all at the expense of just looking outward.

One task of a practitioner is to help people use their imagination more productively. Even when people ruminate excessively, if they do so with *hope* they are less likely to be depressed by their imaginings.[7]

We can also help our clients not just to stop misusing their creativity to catastrophize, but also to sometimes actually *suspend* the use of imagination altogether, especially when situations are ambiguous. (For other ways to help clients manage their emotions, see this blog post.)

But untamed imagination or a failure to find creative meaning can lead to even worse consequences.

Mayhem and murder for kicks

Searingly clever Nathan Freudenthal Leopold Jr. apparently mastered 27 foreign languages. But along with fellow wealthy student Richard Albert Loeb, he murdered 14-year-old Robert Franks in 1924.[8] Their motive?

Creative challenge. To commit 'the perfect murder'.

More recently, British serial killer Joanna Dennehy, supported by her besotted 7-foot-3 boyfriend Gary Stretch (yes, fact is often weirder than fiction!), said she killed to "see how it would feel", adding that murder got "moreish" and she "got a taste for it".[9]

Then there was the case of sadistic killer Mark Riebe, who confessed to killing for kicks,[10] and many other cases besides.

Can I *do* this? Is it possible? Will I get away with it?

Yes, these are extreme examples that represent a tiny minority of offenders, but the same *drive* to cause trouble for the apparent completion of a need for excitement or creative challenge can also be seen in much lesser, but still destructive, actions.

Can I make this person cry? Can I ruin this oh so pleasant meal for everyone by manufacturing a complaint about it? Can I start a row with my spouse?

The need for excitement can smuggle itself, well disguised, into many areas of life. As of course can the need for attention.

You might say being driven to kill as a way of expressing *creativity* is the exclusive realm of the rare malignant psychopath. Yet millions of *non*-psychopaths have killed throughout history for created ideologies. Someone creates the ideology,[11] then others become the avatar for or infected *carrier* of that ideology. Herein lies the power of these ideologies: Their carriers activate its patterns, however destructive.

And how many millions have been crushed under the creative tyranny of visionary utopianists? The need to create is indiscriminate, because creation is deceptively close to destruction – at least among humans. We seem to be the only species with the creativity to kill for sport or ideology.

More prosaically... Shelly, a client, told me she had started shoplifting "for the excitement". Kyle told me he bit his fingernails to shreds when he was bored. Pamela said she'd gotten into the destructive habit of mocking her undemonstrative boyfriend in public for "the buzz". Fian told me he would get drunk and start fights with strangers on nights out just to "feel alive!"

Then there was Philip. He became a millionaire by the age

of 40, and retired. "That's when I started on the cocaine! And now it's got me by the balls! Maybe I need a new creative challenge. I was *happy* when I was working. When I lived on my wits and had to rise to the challenge of building my business."

So it goes.

If we don't create something good, we may be driven to create discord, mayhem or, at the extreme end of the spectrum, murder. Make no mistake, it could happen to you or I – given the right (or wrong) circumstances.

How do your clients meet their needs for challenge and creative outlet? What are they *working* towards?

If we don't find creative meaning, it will find us. But will it really be creative? The creative impulse is too easily mimicked by its evil twin, the *destructive* drive.

In the words of Bob Dylan, *"He not busy being born is busy dying."*

CHAPTER EIGHT

MIND AND BODY

HOW THE DRIVE TO MEET YOUR MIND/BODY NEEDS CAN LEAD TO DISASTER

> *"The human body experiences a powerful gravitational pull in the direction of hope. That is why the patient's hopes are the physician's secret weapon. They are the hidden ingredients in any prescription."*
>
> NORMAN COUSINS

To eat another person. A horrible thought (I'm hoping!). But if you were desperate enough? Sure, I know cannibalism has been a grim practice among some tribes, and the odd, extremely odd, serial killer. But I'm not asking whether you would *want* to eat another person. I'm talking about if there were, or seemed to be, no *other* options.

You're all at sea for months on end, or wandering the Andes after the miracle of surviving a plane crash.[1] You have a physical need, and you *have* to meet it.

But our needs are not just physical.

This whole book is, in a way, about cannibalism. Metaphorically speaking, I hasten to add.

When we feel there is no actual 'food', we might be driven eventually to cannibalism – or we might need to learn what we *can* legitimately eat. We might need to learn to distinguish between real food and fake or poisonous 'food'.

Someone starving for attention may cannibalize a learning situation, for instance, by doing all the talking. They may monopolize and take attention *away* from the teacher and others. By 'eating the wrong thing', they prevent another need from being fulfilled: the need for them and others to learn.

Someone starving for some kind of recognition from his peers might behave badly as a way of gleaning *some* status. Someone starving for the nutrition of intimacy might glean it from some poisonous source such as an abuser or even a kidnapper.

How we meet our needs determines what kind of a world we live in.

If you want to know human motivation, understand emotional problems and recognize how evil operates, then you *have* to appreciate how the drive to meet our basic primal needs can fulfil or destroy us.

In this piece we look how thwarted mind/body needs can play havoc with lives and how trying to meet a desperate physical need in the wrong way can send us spinning into catastrophe.

But first let me tell you about Dave, whose inability to meet a fundamental mind/body need had him balancing precariously on the edge of madness.

What do you say to the Devil when you meet him in the subway?

"I kept thinking that if God exists, then so too must the Devil. And I kept sensing I was about to bump into him. Maybe at the top the stairs, or in the lonely, late-night stillness of a deserted underground station at the bottom of some Godforsaken escalator.

"The weird thing was, I got to thinking... what would, or *should,* I say to him if our paths were to cross? I mean, what's the diabolical etiquette? And one day... there he was. As though waiting for me. A tall gentleman in a Trilby hat..."

Not to sleep perchance to dream

Dave wasn't psychotic in the normal sense. He was sleep deprived. He was under enormous pressure. His house had become worth less than he was paying for it. He'd had to take on two jobs and would "maybe catch 10 minutes of shut-eye here and there". He had four dependent children.

Eventually he crashed (and couldn't work at all for six weeks), but not before begging his hallucinated Prince of Darkness, "Please... I just need to sleep... please let me sleep."

Dave told me he'd actually seen into the evil eyes of his Devil. Though he knew now, and even partly at the time, that he was merely dreaming while awake. If your brain doesn't get enough REM sleep – in Dave's case because he wasn't sleeping at all – then the dream mechanism will start to operate when you are awake.[2]

"The night after I met the Devil in the subway, I collapsed into bed. I slept for 16 solid hours. I felt much better, but still drained."

I wasn't surprised. Dave hadn't been eating properly, but *had* been drinking "up to 30 cups of strong coffee a day".

Your body matters, and so does your mind, because they're the *same* matter. Your emotions directly affect your body, and it goes the other way too.

Our amazing intertwinement

Mental and physical health cannot be disentangled. Dave's sleep starvation had a huge impact on his mental wellbeing.

Dictatorships often use sleep deprivation or physical stress techniques (along with more direct 'interrogation') on members of their hapless populations. The mind is influenced through the body. Body and mind. Mind and body.

Depression is a physical stress condition as much as, or I should say, alongside, an emotional disorder.[3] Its effects can feel as much physical as emotional.

Long-term stress causes inflammation in the body, which in turn contributes to all kinds of diseases.[4] Even the simple act of recalling a time you were really angry can reduce the pumping efficiency of the heart.[5]

Perceived social rejection lights up the same brain regions as the experience of physical pain.[6] On the other side of the coin, viewing a picture of someone you love lessens the impact of physical pain by 44%,[7] and *being* in an emotionally supportive relationship helps both mental and physical health.[89] I could go on (and on), but I won't. You get the idea. What is good for the mind is good for the body.

And what is good for the body is good for the mind. Having a terrible diet (or eating foods your body is intolerant of) can make you feel depressed and anxious.[10] Conversely, physical exercise is protective against anxiety[11] and a wonderful mood enhancer,[12] especially when done outdoors in nature.[13]

We all understand that attempting to assuage thirst through drinking engine oil is a terrible idea. Yet you will have seen clients, and perhaps loved ones too, attempt to do something very similar.

What are your relationships with?

Michelle had been eating a large chocolate bar every night for around a year. I asked her if anything had happened a year ago, and she told me it had. Her relationship had broken down. She wasn't slow to recognize that this was all an unconscious attempt at meeting her need for intimacy.

Michelle had a relationship with chocolate. Many of us do have *some* kind of relationship with sugar, or caffeine, or drugs, or chocolate. But these are stop gaps.

There is a very real part of all of us that knows full well that a relationship with alcohol or drugs or sweet pastry pies is no real substitute for a warm loving romance or friendship, or for a life rich in meaning or social connection.

But in the moment it can *feel* like a solution. Just as, for a few seconds, eating cardboard may feel like a solution when we are starving. But if there *were* real food to find and we knew how to gain it, why even think about eating the cardboard?

When your client is abusing themselves in some way, whether through smoking out their poor lungs, 'comfort eating' (which has been shown to not even provide comfort!)[14], or any other destructive behaviour, it's vital to discover just what they *really* need. And of course help them meet that need (or needs) legitimately.

Intolerable side effects

It's a cliché to talk about 'self-medicating'. But people do. Whether through alcohol, or barbiturates, or cannabis, it's a common way to 'switch off', forget about the day and absorb oneself in the moment.

But self-medication is always accompanied by self-delusion – convincing ourselves, consciously or unconsciously, that the 'medication' has few side effects, or that somehow we can cheat the future.

Cliché it may be, but 'self-medication' is a fine analogy. Indeed, it's the *side effects* that are the problem. Side effects that can make it harder for people to meet their *actual* physical and emotional needs.

When we seek in the long term to provide ourselves with energy through coffee instead of rest, to distract ourselves from problems through the oblivion of drugs, or to resort to any form of self-harm rather than actually working to solve our problems, then the attempted 'solution' becomes the enemy – not the comforting or encouraging 'friend' it might masquerade as.

And, at the real risk of sounding like a bearded, wind-chimey man sitting next to you in a Peruvian hippy sweat lodge, there's something else.

Listen and you will hear

We all need to work at being attuned to our bodies. If we don't, we can lose the capacity to interpret the signals from our bodies. We need to *listen* to our bodies – always. What is it you actually need?

Each and every one of us has a natural current running through us called the ultradian rhythm. Every 90 to 120 minutes we shift from left-brain dominance to right-brain. The shift takes about 20 minutes, and it usually makes us feel a little entranced or daydreamy.

This is the time at work we might feel like just stopping for a chat. Maybe we need to just slow down for a little while, or shift from outward to inward focus. But too many of us try to override the feeling with more coffee or a crafty cigarette. We silence the body's attempts to let us know what we need. Or we just refuse to listen.

It's during this shift that the immune system does its upkeep, the brain incorporates new learning, and the gut digests and absorbs nutrients. It's little wonder that when we continue to swim against the tides of this natural rhythm we start to feel broken and emotional.

Sure, you can refuse to listen to your physical needs for a while, override them for a bit... but do it for long enough and you'll come to feel depleted on every level.

I see the shift in ultradian rhythm in my clients sometimes. It's as if a ray of light has altered their features when someone who has been very outward focused suddenly becomes glassy eyed. Their breathing naturally changes and slows. Their jaw slackens. Sometimes I even hear their tummy rumble as they digest food.

And *that's* when they more easily travel inward. Hypnotizing someone is often a case of just letting the sails catch the breeze of this warm and wonderful natural shift in physical and mental focus.

We need to listen and work *with,* not against ourselves.

I not robot!

People increasingly treat themselves as machines. We work through lunch, sleep too little, eat junk on the run, skip the gym, and prop up our flagging bodies with 'energy drinks'.

But neglecting proper nutrition, sleep, rest, and exercise long term leads to psychological problems and stress-induced illness, and not just on the individual level. In unhealthy populations, collective emotions run riot. And that can lead us down some dark paths.

With too little exposure to natural light, poor nutrition, and scant exercise we start to feel second-rate. Weak and sick in mind and body.

But the very ways we try to *meet* our physical needs for activity, energy, and relaxation can leave us with a 'cure' even worse than the 'disease'.

We all need to stop cannibalizing ourselves.

CHAPTER NINE
MEANING

HOW THE DIVERTED DRIVE FOR MEANING CAN WREAK HAVOC IN OUR LIVES

> *"The word 'happy' would lose its meaning if it were not balanced by sadness."*
>
> CARL JUNG

Without meaning we depress. With no purpose we wither. We fade far from who we *might* be. But think of the reverse.

When our lives feel *meaningful* we are energized and focused. Even suffering is made more bearable.

We live in times in which many people feel meaningless. Many of the old coherent belief structures, such as organized religion, have fragmented and diminished. We have, it seems, fewer providers of ready-made meaning.

As well, many of the 'secular religions' such as communism have lost their appeal, certainly in the countries that had to live and die under them.

Cynicism seems epidemic. Suicide rates[1], especially among young men, continue to climb.[2] We have entertainment aplenty. Distraction in spades. Material promise in abundance. But *meaning*?

The holy search for happiness

Religions, including secular ones, were and are about being pious rather than becoming or being personally happy.

Follow the dictates of this or that religion and you will become good and acceptable. *Serve* the holy tenets of this or that belief system to derive your meaning.

I'm not saying whether religion or any of the major political belief systems are true, but they certainly do and did provide people with a sense of purpose and meaning.

As religion has declined, in recent times the idea of 'being happy' *as a goal in itself* has become ingrained in our culture. Live for yourself![3]

But happiness is often seen not as a *byproduct* of meeting needs, or as an oscillating state of mind, but as some constant future state which will, once arrived at, persist forever. Oh really?

To give is to get

Perhaps the drive to 'be happy' or 'be successful' has replaced a sense of service to a greater cause. Or, I should say, the part that serving a greater cause played in making people happier has been replaced by the idea that we can make ourselves directly happier without meeting our needs in balance.

This is in part, maybe in large part, due to mass and massive consumerism. But seeking to meet one's own greeds above needs doesn't seem to make people particularly happy. Actually, quite the reverse.[4]

The problem is that it's hard to maintain a sense of strong

meaning just by fulfilling personal financial or material goals. Or, in fact, by just focusing on the self. Sure, you might look great or have money to burn and a house to envy. But then what? What next?

Making idols of demons

It's been said that if we make an idol of something that *doesn't have the qualities of a god* we and others will inevitably suffer.

Trying to find meaning from inadequate sources will not work long term. In fact, the search to feel meaningful might have us flitting around like a crazed honeybee in an artificial flower factory.

One client, Derek, told me how he had constantly moved house because he felt the "grass was always greener on the other side". He had been a communist (which I thought might have conflicted with his serial private property ownership!), a libertarian, a Catholic, and lately a fitness fanatic.

Each new enthusiasm was meant to make his life meaningful. But it never quite did. He had made money and didn't need to work but felt, he told me, "empty". Derek epitomized the paradox of a search for meaning.

Whom are we doing this for?

Paradoxically, unless we serve something for *its* sake and not for ours, then meaning will shrink even as we try to approach it.

People often suddenly find their lives are filled with meaning when they acquire responsibility. Perhaps they have children or adopt a worthy cause. Or they suddenly feel needed in some other way.

I recall hearing about a project in a school in which antisocial older boys were asked to be responsible and mentor disaffected younger ones. The result? Apparently the younger boys benefited from the mentoring, but not as much as the older boys, who often relished their newfound responsibility and suddenly discovered a sense of meaning.

Perhaps responsibility should be a human right!

Mind you, it does seem kind of old fashioned to talk of the value of service. But that's really what responsibility and meaning... err... mean.

Serving but not subservient

When we are responsible for something, we *serve* it, and it becomes more of a focus than we ourselves are. Manageable responsibility is wonderful for mental health. To feel needed helps us live longer and feel happier because of the *meaning* the responsibility gives us.[5]

But unless what we worship has the qualities of a god, then religious-like, fervent belief in it may just be a cul de sac. The Nazis worshipped at the altar of their 'religion' and derived a huge sense of meaning from their divisive identity politics. But the idol they worshipped most certainly did not have the qualities of a god.

Fitness is great, but its worship can't meet as many needs as a more all-encompassing faith or focus. It's never going to provide *all* meaning. Derek had been trying to find a basket for all his eggs, and fitness wasn't about to provide it.

Meaning, or excitement?

For Derek, meaning was synonymous with excitement, and excitement is really just another word for entertainment. Once the excitement of the current meaning-making device wore off, so did his commitment to it. Excitement without responsibility can't provide a sense of meaning long term.

Indeed, as time passed, the latest focus never quite felt as meaningful as he had assumed or hoped. He would find rationales to explain why it wasn't the right path for him after all. But he couldn't quite see the *wider* problem.

He was flitting from one thing to the next in an ineffective search for meaning.

It wasn't necessarily *Derek's* approach that was misaligned, but the different dietary, fitness or political creeds he kept attaching to.

"If I can just live here or do that, then this hole in my heart where a sense of meaning should be will be gloriously and eternally filled!"

He was trying to worship idols that didn't have the qualities of gods.

So you become the fittest man or woman alive. Then what?

We can *find* meaning, or we can make it. We can glean it from different sources, or we can find it mainly in one place. And it's a *byproduct* of meeting our needs. But we can also fabricate it from something that doesn't really supply it well, or for long, or widely enough.

So what is this 'meaningful' experience that so many people seem to be searching for? What does it feel like to have a sense of meaning?

Meaning making

When you have a sense of meaning you feel galvanized. Energized.

It's cold? You're tired? You've been invited to a party that you'd like to attend? It's raining? It's too early in the morning to get yourself out of bed?

No matter to any of that!

You have something to *do*! And circumstances and perhaps other people depend on you. The something to do is more important than any of these lower considerations. A wider sense of meaning stops us being simply a bloated bag of appetites blown around by our immediate and fluctuating whims.

People who procrastinate may tell you that the thing they are *not* doing is "really meaningful" to them. But words are not actions. And we should watch what people do as well as say. We learn what others and ourselves are like by seeing what they and we *actually* do.

Serving a higher need

Meaning makes you feel not that you don't matter at all, but rather that the meaning you serve is of *greater* importance – at least in the moment. Meaning also helps you feel integral to the responsibility of serving that meaning.

We need meaning, and when we don't find it we *make* it if we can. We can find meaning in family, friends, work, creative challenge, and serving a wider purpose.

We may be encouraged subconsciously to find meaning from material products. But that's akin to trying to fill up a bucket with a bucket-sized hole in it.

A sense of meaning doesn't eliminate suffering. But it can contextualize it. Learning generates meaning and so does truth seeking. And meaning and personal comfort don't necessarily track alongside one another.

But there's another problem, perhaps larger than incessant materialism.

Nothing really matters

The rise of postmodern relativism,[6] in which it is believed there are no *truths* but only *perspectives*, may have led to less fulfilment of the need for meaning. This is such an embedded idea that it may even seem absurd to point out that it is *just* an idea.

If there *are* no ultimate meanings then why bother? If everything is just a social construct, and the meaning of bad actions is no different than the meaning of good actions, then it matters not what you do or what you (don't) take responsibility for.

But without a strong sense of meaning, which comes from making value judgements, having challenges and rising to them, meeting your needs in balance, *and* having a sense that you are serving some greater truth, or at least trying to, life feels pointless. A circular trudge rather than an exciting and fulfilling journey.

What I've tried to do

In this book, I've tried to illustrate how thwarted and disastrously diverted primal emotional needs can be. How trying to meet needs blindly or from negative sources can have terrible consequences. Being so 'thirsty' that you'll even drink engine oil happens all the time on the emotional level.

We've looked at how the need for attention can become so great that clients will even try to meet it in ways that emotionally poison them. We've seen how the needs for a sense of control, status, intimacy, challenge, connection and safety can, when the need is met desperately and blindly, lead to some terrible places.

We've also seen how the thwarted and misplaced drive to

meet the needs of the mind/body system can make us mad and sad.

Inevitably, because meeting needs produces that all-important sense of meaning, I have talked about meaning before. The meaning for me in writing this book is that so many people still seem unaware of how forcefully these unconscious drives to meet these needs affect them.

And also how *without* this self-knowledge we can assume we are doing one thing while really simply trying to meet a basic emotional need that might be better met elsewhere.

Here are a few ways in which the need for meaning can be subverted badly and damage your clients and loved ones.

But it means so much to me!

Relationships matter, and provide more meaning than wealth alone.[7] People seem keener to escape smoking because they appreciate how it might drag them through the gates of death *away from time on Earth spent with loved ones* rather than because they want to save money.

But if someone gets *all* their meaning from romantic relationships then, because of the vicissitudinal nature of relationships, they may be cruising for an emotional bruising.

If having a relationship is, to them, the *ultimate* meaning, then different things can go wrong. Maybe they become *so* focused on the relationship that they start to over-monitor it. If all their meaning is derived from this one area, they may become insecure and needy to the point of destroying the only source of their meaning.

Deriving all meaning from just one other person can be as bad as trying to derive it through pure focus on the self.

Looking for meaning in the wrong places

If responsibility is lacking and we place all meaning and importance on the self, and the fulfilment of its wants, this may never feel meaningful enough – because that's not how meaning works.

Remember Derek, flitting from one new enthusiasm to another, but never to one that helped the *wider* community.

And of course, sometimes what *should* (because it concerns the welfare of others) be meaningful to us is squeezed out by what we might call trivial areas of life (yes, I know that was a value judgement – see my comments about postmodern relativism above!).

Neglecting more meaningful parts of life

Some people may derive their *primary* sense of meaning from a source that doesn't really nourish them or others. One client's greatest meaning was met through the fortunes of his chosen sports team. The problem was that he was neglecting other, more truly meaningful parts of his life: his wife and children and work.

Lastly, because meaning is such an overarching need, some of us may glean it from a malevolent, parasitic, or even deadly source. Especially when we are desperate for the life-transforming effect of meaning.

When the price is too high

We may be abused by the person we are in that *meaningful* relationship with, if we invest so much meaning in it that the abuse becomes the price we feel we have to pay.

The Jim Jones cult[8] provided those starved for meaning with plenty of meaning. They were going to help save the world! What greater meaning could there be?

But the price was plenty of abuse and death. Isis and Nazism and communism and David Koresh's cult at Waco and drugs and alcohol and extreme sports and the game of Russian roulette have all provided meaning – and destruction.

When we are starving, unless we understand the nature of 'real food', we may eat anything, even poison. I think humanity perhaps more than ever needs to truly and clearly understand its own needs. Not just to avoid catastrophe but to fulfil our vast potential. We need to understand ourselves and others so that we can work together for the real betterment of us all.

I hope you have enjoyed reading this book on The Dark Side of Your Emotional Needs as much as I have enjoyed writing it.

NOTES

I. Attention

1. http://journals.lww.com/psychosomaticmedicine/Abstract/2002/05000/Loneliness_and_Health__Potential_Mechanisms.5.aspx

III. Control

1. http://onlinelibrary.wiley.com/doi/10.1111/j.1559-1816.1999.tb00133.x/full
2. http://www.tandfonline.com/doi/full/10.1080/01634372.2016.1267672
3. http://onlinelibrary.wiley.com/doi/10.1111/j.1540-4560.1991.tb01832.x/full
4. http://www.sciencedirect.com/science/article/pii/S0885392498800080
5. http://psycnet.apa.org/record/1988-35828-001
6. http://psycnet.apa.org/record/1975-10978-001
7. http://onlinelibrary.wiley.com/doi/10.1111/jopy.12333/abstract
8. http://onlinelibrary.wiley.com/doi/10.1002/erv.605/full

IV. Intimacy

1. https://www.ncbi.nlm.nih.gov/pubmed/16330726

V. Connection

1. Mussolini, who had a Jewish mistress and friends, famously said: "Race? It is a feeling, not a reality. ... National pride has no need of the delirium of race."
2. Williams, K. D., Forgas, J. P., and von Hippel, W. (Eds) (2005), *The social outcast: Ostracism, social exclusion, rejection, and bullying.* Psychology Press, New York.
3. https://academic.oup.com/scan/article/6/2/234/1617474/Responses-to-ostracism-across-adulthood
4. http://www.columbia.edu/~nb2229/docs/bolger-zuckerman-kessler-jpsp-2000.pdf

5. https://www.sciencedaily.com/releases/2014/06/140612104950.htm
6. For a wonderful clarification of cultishness in everyday life, see: Deikman, A. (1990), *The wrong way home: Uncovering the patterns of cult behavior in American society*. Beacon Press, Boston.
7. Milgram, S. (1973), 'The perils of obedience'. Published in *Harper's Magazine*, December 1973.
8. https://en.wikipedia.org/wiki/Gustave_Le_Bon
9. https://www.sciencedaily.com/releases/2014/06/140612104950.htm

VI. Status

1. https://www.health.harvard.edu/press_releases/oscar_winners
2. https://en.wikipedia.org/wiki/Whitehall_Study
3. https://www.ncbi.nlm.nih.gov/pmc/articles/PMC2837459/
4. http://www.pnas.org/content/109/17/6490.abstract
5. http://psycnet.apa.org/journals/psp/28/1/129/
6. https://en.wikipedia.org/wiki/Stanford_prison_experiment
7. See: http://sheilaisenberg.com/women-who-love-men-who-kill-2/

VII. Challenge

1. See Howard, P. J., Ph.D., The owner's manual for the brain. pp. 25–26, 726. GA: Bard Press, 1994, 2000. See also Eysenck, H. J., The biological basis of personality. Springfield, IL: Thomas, 1967.
2. See Carr, N., The shallows: What the internet is doing to our brains. NY: W. W. Norton & Company, 2010.
3. https://www.cmu.edu/dietrich/sds/docs/loewenstein/BoredUSA.pdf
4. http://journals.sagepub.com/doi/abs/10.2466/pr0.1992.70.3.688
5. See: https://www.hgi.org.uk/useful-information/schizophrenia-and-psychosis
6. http://www.bbc.co.uk/news/magazine-24444431
7. https://ijmhs.biomedcentral.com/articles/10.1186/1752-4458-8-53
8. Alfred Hitchcock's (almost) one-take 1948 movie 'Rope' was based on the Leopold and Loeb case. See also https://en.wikipedia.org/wiki/Leopold_and_Loeb
9. http://courtnewsuk.co.uk/joanna-dennehy-killing-for-kicks/
10. https://www.mirror.co.uk/news/world-news/piers-morgan-face-face-mass-11529260
11. See Solzhenitsyn, A., The Gulag Archipelago. Paris, France: Éditions du Seuil, 1973.

VIII. Mind and Body

1. https://en.wikipedia.org/wiki/Uruguayan_Air_Force_Flight_571#Cannibalism
2. http://journals.sagepub.com/doi/abs/10.2466/pms.1989.68.3.787, http://onlinelibrary.wiley.com/doi/10.1111/j.1749-6632.1962.tb50101.x/full
3. Nemeroff, C. B. (1998) The neurobiology of depression. *Scientific American*, 278, 6, 28–35.
4. https://www.sciencedaily.com/releases/2012/04/120402162546.htm
5. In one study (https://www.sciencedirect.com/science/article/pii/000291499290605X) conducted at Stanford Medical School, heart patients were asked to recall times when they had been angry. Although, according to the patients, the anger they felt on recalling the events was only half as strong as it had been during the original experience, their hearts started pumping, on average, 5% less efficiently. Cardiologists view a 7% drop in pumping efficiency as serious enough to cause a heart attack. See also https://link.springer.com/article/10.1023/A:1005596208324
6. http://www.pnas.org/content/108/15/6270.long
7. http://journals.plos.org/plosone/article?id=10.1371/journal.pone.0013309
8. https://www.medicalnewstoday.com/articles/233278.php
9. http://journals.sagepub.com/doi/abs/10.1177/0265407505056438
10. https://www.nature.com/articles/s41598-017-05649-7
11. https://www.ncbi.nlm.nih.gov/pubmed/22895382
12. https://www.sciencedirect.com/science/article/pii/S0163834317300476?via%3Dihub
13. https://www.sciencedirect.com/science/article/pii/S0272494409000838?via%3Dihub
14. http://psycnet.apa.org/doiLanding?doi=10.1037%2Fhea0000068

IX. Meaning

1. https://www.befrienders.org/suicide-statistics
2. https://www.ncbi.nlm.nih.gov/pmc/articles/PMC1414751/#!po=31.0811
3. See Adam Curtis's documentary *The Century of The Self*: https://en.wikipedia.org/wiki/The_Century_of_the_Self
4. http://www.medicaldaily.com/materialism-makes-people-unhappy-what-focus-instead-297376
5. http://www.ucl.ac.uk/news/news-articles/1114/061114-longer-lifespan
6. https://en.wikipedia.org/wiki/Relativism#Postmodernism_and_relativism
7. https://voxeu.org/article/origins-happiness
8. https://en.wikipedia.org/wiki/Jim_Jones

RESOURCES

You can find additional resources on this topic, as well as all of the links from the endnotes, here: https://unk.com/darkside.

A REQUEST

If you enjoyed this book, it would help me greatly if you would review it online wherever you purchased it. A review can make all the difference for the book's visibility and helps other readers discover new books.

Thank you!

FREE THERAPY TECHNIQUES

Get free therapy techniques every week to use with your very next client. Join the 77,134+ practitioners who receive an uncommon article every week with the latest therapy techniques.

If you are a practitioner any persuasion; counsellor, psychotherapist, hypnotherapist, life coach, bodyworker, in fact anyone who works in the helping professions, you will glean valuable, actionable ideas, tips and techniques from Clear Thinking.

Join over 77,134 subscribers receiving articles on topics such as depression, anxiety, OCD, PTSD and more. All delivered to you on a weekly basis as a short, punchy article.

You will also receive video presentations, live therapy footage and subscriber-only offers for our training courses.

Subscribe to our free therapy techniques newsletter today and you will be sent my reframing eBook *New Ways of Seeing* right away!

Sign up here: https://www.unk.com/blog/free-therapy-techniques/.

TRAIN ONLINE WITH MARK TYRRELL

We provide online therapy skills training courses in Uncommon U. These are highly practical, video-supported training with video of real clients sessions, demonstrations with actors and multiple formats (if you prefer to read than listen/watch for example).

Uncommon Knowledge has been training practitioners since 1999, and online since 2007. Our courses are known for being focused, practical and easy to learn from. Our goal is to ensure you finish the course with new skills that you know how to apply with your very next client. (Not to bury you in information!)

Some courses are available all the time, some periodically. On the course description pages below you will be able to register your interest for any course that is not currently open for booking. All types of practitioners take our courses, from counsellors to life coaches, cognitive-behavioural therapists to psychologists, hypnotherapists to social workers. We'll see you inside!

Learn more here: https://www.unk.com/blog/courses/.

ABOUT MARK TYRRELL

Mark Tyrrell is a therapist, author and psychology educator. Since founding Uncommon Knowledge with Roger Elliott in 1998, Mark has penned more than a million words on psychology and philosophy, delivered a Diploma in Solution-Focused Psychotherapy for ten years, authored his reframing book New Ways of Seeing, co-authored The Giant Within, and created over 500 hours of self-help videos.

He currently writes a blog at Uncommon Practitioners - https://www.unk.com/blog - where he also delivers online training which is enjoyed by health professionals of all disciplines. Since they first went online in 1999, more than a million people have subscribed to Mark's online courses, and over 100 million have visited Uncommon Knowledge's psychology and therapy websites.

When he has a spare moment, Mark enjoys playing tennis and training in obscure martial arts.

facebook.com/uncommonknowledge
twitter.com/unktweets
instagram.com/marktyrrellunk
linkedin.com/in/mark-tyrrell
amazon.com/Mark-Tyrrell/e/B001H9PBL6
bookbub.com/profile/mark-tyrrell

ALSO BY MARK TYRRELL

New Ways of Seeing: The Art of Therapeutic Reframing: How to use your words to release your clients from limiting beliefs, including examples from 81 real cases.

Uncommon Practitioners Series

PTSD: Horror in the Mind: The psychology of post-traumatic stress disorder, and the ethical way to lift it

Printed in Great Britain
by Amazon

16464980R00079